Y0-BXK-290

248.4   11594   c.1
Hea

    Heagle, John
        Our journey toward

248.4
Hea   11594
                                    c.1
        Heagle, John
            Our journey
          toward God.

OUR
JOURNEY
TOWARD
GOD

OUR
JOURNEY
TOWARD
GOD

by
John Heagle

Novitiate Library
Mont La Salle
Napa, California

THE THOMAS MORE PRESS
Chicago, Illinois

11594

Permission to use Published Material

The author wishes to thank the following for permission to quote material from these publications.

Excerpts from the Jerusalem Bible, Copyright 1966 by Darton, Longman and Todd, Ltd. and Doubleday Company, Inc. Used by permission of the publisher.

Lines from *A Sleep of Prisoners*, by Christopher Fry as found in *Three Plays*. Hesperides book edition. Oxford University Press, New York, 1961, p. 209. Used by permission of the publisher.

Excerpt from *Letters from a Traveller*, by Teilhard de Chardin. Harper and Row, Publishers, New York & Evanston, 1962, p. 101. Used by permission of the Publisher.

Excerpt from "The Memorial," by Blaise Pascal. As found in *The Essential Pascal*. Edited by Robert W. Gleason, Trans. by G. F. Pullen. New American Library, Mentor-Omega Books, 1966, p. 205. Used by permission of the publisher.

Lines from "Reluctance," from *The Poetry of Robert Frost*, edited by Edward Connery Lathem. Copyright © 1942 by Robert Frost, Copyright © 1969 by Holt, Rinehart and Winston, Inc. Copyright © 1970 by Lesley Frost Ballantine. Reprinted by permission of Holt, Rinehart & Winston, Inc.

Lines from "East Coker" in *Four Quartets* by T. S. Eliot, copyright 1943 by T. S. Eliot; copyright, 1971 by Esme Valerie Eliot. Reprinted by permission of Harcourt Brace Jovanovich, Inc.

Excerpt from *St. Francis*, by Nikos Kanzantzakis. Trans. by P. A. Bien (New York: Simon & Schuster, Touchstone Books, 1962), p. 187. Used by permission of the publisher.

Copyright © 1977 by The Thomas More Association. All rights reserved. Printed in the United States of America. No part of this publication may be reproduced, stored in a retrieval system, or transmitted, in any form or by any means, electronic, mechanical, photocopying, recording, or otherwise, without the prior written permission of the publisher, The Thomas More Association, 180 North Wabash, Chicago, Illinois 60601.

ISBN 0-88347-071-3

CONTENTS

To the Easter People in my life

ACKNOWLEDGMENTS

To write is to struggle with a vision. It is the search to find words for one's life. In writing this book, I have discovered in a new and deeper way how much I need other people. I want to acknowledge some of those who have struggled with the vision and who have shared the journey.

I want to thank Sister Paula Ripple, F.S.P.A., for her creative help in editing the manuscript. Her friendship and vision have been invaluable.

I also want to express my gratitude to the students, the faculty, and the administrators of Viterbo College. My life is richer and deeper because of the community which I shared with them.

In particular, I want to thank Sister Fran Ferder F.S.P.A. for her friendship and her support.

I am also grateful to Sister Laurian Pieterek, F.S.P.A., for her friendship and understanding.

I want to acknowledge and thank Mrs. Jean Bastian, who typed most of the manuscript, and the community of Holy Family Parish, who have welcomed me into their midst.

Finally, I want to express my gratitude to my family, especially my mother and father, who have continued to encourage me to write.

7

INTRODUCTION

Beneath the confusion and the uncertainty of our age there is a hunger which will not die. In the midst of change and upheaval there is a restlessness which cannot be ignored. The hunger is the quest for God. The restlessness is the search for spirituality.

This book is an exploration of these creative stirrings of the Spirit in our time. It is an attempt to rediscover the underlying vision of the gospel. It is a search for an integrating vision of faith. It is a meditation on Christianity as a way of life.

I have written these reflections out of two basic convictions. First, I believe that the most urgent need in the Church today is the call to live a deeper inward life—the life of the Spirit. Secondly, I am convinced that this spirituality must be rooted in the saving journey of Jesus—his life, death, and resurrection. The Church refers to this journey and our participation in it as the "paschal mystery." The paschal mystery is the central experience of Christian life.

The renewal which was initiated by the Second Vatican Council was, from the beginning, a call to inner conversion. It was a challenge to see more clearly and to live more deeply. In order to create the setting in which this inward renewal could take place, it was necessary to refocus the faith of the Church by revising the forms of liturgical worship and the sacramental rites. It was also necessary to reshape the structure and style of the Church's presence in the world. Many of the new forms of worship and the revised sacramental rites are now available and in use. Some of the most needed structural reforms are under way. Others, hopefully, are still to come.

But these external reforms are only the beachhead of renewal; they are not the renewal itself. If the enthusiasm for reform has faltered, it is because we have not developed the inward vision which is necessary to give meaning to the outward changes. We have revised the rites and the structures, but we have not always touched the transforming energy and vision of the gospel.

The most obvious example of this is related to the paschal mystery. This mystery is at the heart of Christian faith. It is the unspoken context out of which many of the Council documents were written. The paschal mystery is the background for most of the recent liturgical reforms, including the revision of the lectionary. It is the focal point of the new sacramental rites and of the new rite of Christian initiation for adults. Yet, despite all this, the paschal mystery as an integrating vision of spirituality is largely unfamiliar to most Catholics and Christians. The central experience of our faith is, in many instances, not a vital part of our spiritual growth.

I have written this book with the hope that it might be helpful to ordinary Christians in their search to understand their lives as a personal participation in the passover journey of Jesus. Christianity is not, ultimately, a way of explaining life; it is a way of living it. These reflections explore the challenge of what it means for us to be "Followers of the Way."

Chapter One

AS THE WATCHMAN WAITS FOR DAWN

Reading the Signs of the Times

"Son of man, I have appointed you
as sentry to the House of Israel."

Ezk 3:17

The Watchful Tree

It is the time of waiting. Like the sleep of death, the dry season still rules the land. The scorching winds from the Arabah have subsided. There is a stillness at the edge of the desert. As it has done for unremembered seasons, the Judeaen countryside waits for life to stir.

Jeremiah, man of God, waits along with the earth. He has heard the call of God in his life, a call that is both affirming and frightening. He has responded like a child who is suddenly asked to become an adult. He has fretted about his limitations and struggled with his fears. He has wrestled with his inability to speak and with his dread of conflict. He has run out of excuses. Like the world around him, Jeremiah waits for life to stir. He lingers in the shadows of his fears. He can taste the dry soil of his soul.

11

In the afternoon there is rain and the first smell of wet earth. Jeremiah knows that the moment is near. He goes for a walk.

In the barren hillsides not far from Jerusalem, a fresh rainshower has moved off to the east. In the sun, tiny buds, with water still glistening on them, are standing upright, like sentinels, on the branches of a tree.

Jeremiah knows that it is time. "The word of Yahweh was addressed to me asking, 'Jeremiah, what do you see?' 'I see a branch of the Watchful Tree,' I answered. Then Yahweh said, 'Well seen! I too watch over my word to see it fulfilled' " (Jr 1:11-12).

Sheqed is the Hebrew word for "watchful." It is also the name given to the almond tree, the first tree to blossom in a new season. The buds of the almond tree stand straight up on the branch when they appear. Their flowering is an announcement. It is as though they are standing on tiptoe, scanning the horizon for other signs of spring. They strain toward the promise of growth. They are eager for life, as they reach higher for more of the sun's light and warmth.

The almond tree is the sentinel of spring. It is the herald of new life. It is nature's own watchman.

The Watchful Tree is also a living parable. It is written in the language of the earth and spoken in the outlines of life. It reveals both the faithfulness of God and the role of the prophet. Yahweh points to the almond tree as proof of his constancy and fidelity in carrying out his promises. The Lord is the watchman of life for his people. His word is more than a human promise. It is a creative energy which accomplishes all that it sets about doing. "I too watch over my word to see it fulfilled." These words echo a similar commitment which the Lord made to Isaiah: "Yes, as the rain and the snow come down from the heavens and do not return without watering the earth, making it yield and giving growth to provide seed for the sower and bread for the eating, so the word that goes from my mouth does not return to me empty, without carrying out my will and succeeding in what it was sent to do" (Is 55:10-11).

The Watchful Tree also symbolizes the call and the mission of the prophet. This experience of awareness in the world of nature is Jeremiah's first prophetic encounter after his call and consecration by the Lord. What does it reveal to us? It points to the first steps in all spirituality: the receptivity of the heart, and the awareness of life through the eyes of faith. God is indicating that the first task of the prophet is not to speak out, to confront or to act. It is rather a summons to become more aware, to heighten one's consciousness of the presence of God's word in the midst of life.

Jeremiah, what do you see? The prophetic vocation is a call to look and to listen, to see and to hear the Spirit that moves within us and around us. The role of the prophet is to be the Watchful Tree for the people. The sentinel of spring. The herald of life. The watchman of the seasons of history.

What Do You See?

What do you see? Yahweh asks this question not only of Jeremiah, but of all of us as well. It is the challenge he issues to people of faith in every age. It is especially significant for us today, for, like Jeremiah, we are in a season of waiting, a time of expectancy. We have been called to a new vision of the gospel. We have heard a new summons to live the Christian way of life. We have moved through a season of transition in the Church. We have been active in changing the structures and directions of religious experience.

But the renewal, like the early rain, has come only in hints and promises. Something tells us that it is now time. In the winter of our search we look for signs of spring. The signs are all around us. The first buds of spiritual renewal are appearing. Like Jeremiah, our first task is to look with the eyes of faith. The rain stirs us to awareness. We are called to be watchmen. The sentinels of spring.

What do you see? This appears to be a simple question, one involving only the powers of observation and competent reporting. But it is not that simple. The question probes beyond the flood of surface information in search of an underlying vision. What demands does this question make on us? How can we begin to respond to the Lord's challenge in our time?

If the worth of our lives were focused primarily on technological ability, our society might well be considered the most advanced in history. Our powers of observation have multiplied beyond our expectations. We monitor aspects of life that Jeremiah could never have imagined. Millions devote their entire lives to the business of research and analysis. We have developed sophisticated equipment which enables us to observe everything from subatomic particles to distant galaxies. The data from this research is fed through computers and analyzed by experts. It is recorded on microfilm and stored in memory banks. It is made available to multitudes of people in a relatively short time. It flows into libraries and journals, into scientific publications and conferences. It becomes part of an expanding information explosion.

Once, "The Eyes and Ears of the World" was a weekly news review at the local movie theater. Now the eyes and ears of the world look at us and listen to us from the other side of the moon. The night sky is alive with satellites that circle the earth. Radar networks monitor our borders. X-rays probe the organic functions of our bodies. We have developed sophisticated surveillance equipment. We have burglar alarms for our banks and for our homes. We tap telephones and tape conversations. We measure the tremors of the earth and follow the storm systems from weather satellites. Some of us watch thousands of hours of television a year. We see European political developments and the Olympic games live, via Telstar. We listen numbly as the evening news reports a scientific breakthrough in the makeup of the gene. We switch channels as a remote-

controlled camera sends back near-perfect
pictures of soil sampling on Mars. We might ask
ourselves: What do we *see*? Our answers would
describe a flood of information, news, research
charts, opinion polls, Dow Jones averages, and
defense statistics.

Technologically, we are the most observant and
informed people in history. But what do we really
see? Is there a vision or a direction for the human
spirit in the midst of it all? Despite the sophis-
tication with which we now study our world, there
remains a lingering sense of confusion, an underlying feeling of bewilderment. We have a multi-
tude of data, but we don't know what to do with
it. We have the facts and the statistics, but we
lack the inner vision to understand the burden and
the promise of our age. It is one thing to gather
data. It is another to view life, to hear its deeper
pulse, and to understand its flow and direction
in relation to God. We monitor the weather systems, and predict the temperatures and local
conditions, but we do not understand the climate
of the times, the inner weather of the human
spirit.

Jesus confronted the people of his age with this
same challenge. "When you see a cloud looming
up in the West you say at once that rain is coming,
and so it does. And when the wind is from the
south you say it will be hot, and it is. Hypocrites!
You know how to interpret the face of the earth
and the sky. How is it you do not know how to
interpret these times" (Lk 12:54-56)?

God gave Jeremiah the challenge of interpreting
the times and of reading the inner weather of the
spirit. He gives us the same mission today. This
task is not merely academic or theoretical. The
future of human awareness and creativity are at
stake. The possibility of faith and the vision of the
spirit hang in the balance.

A few years ago a popular weekly magazine ran
a double page ad for IBM. It pictured a man sitting
on a rock and looking out over the sea. The caption
beneath it read: "No one can take the ultimate
weight of decision-making off your shoulders. But
the more you know about how things really are,
the lighter the burden will be." At the bottom of
the ad, in small print, were these words: "IBM.
Not just data, reality."

IBM advertisers have summarized what some in
our society consider to be the essence of "seeing."
The willingness to assist the human community in
the task of processing information is commend-
able, but the assertion that computers can go
beyond data to give us reality is dangerous and
deceptive. Data is not the same as reality. The
confusion of the two has created a crisis in our
understanding of truth. Data is necessary in help-
ing us to describe reality. It gives us important
information about it. But reality is deeper than
any computer printout. When the data that describes life is exalted as reality, we are in danger
of losing the mystery and vision of life. We cut life
off from the creative roots in which the spirit of
scientific inquiry was born. Science cannot ignore

its roots in mystery without cutting itself off from reality.

The circumstances of history and the level of technological development may be different, but the question which Jeremiah heard in his life is still as urgent today. What do you *see?* That question is ultimately addressed to the human heart, not to a calculator. If we transfer the quest for vision to the careful, controlled search for facts, we will set aside that which makes us unique in all the universe—our search for God in the midst of human life. We would begin to fit the psalmists' description of the idols of his day:

> "Do the pagans ask, 'Where is their God?'
> Ours is the God whose will is sovereign
> in the heavens and on earth,
> whereas their idols, in silver and gold,
> products of human skill,
>
> have mouths, but never speak,
> eyes, but never see,
> ears, but never hear,
> noses, but never smell,
>
> hands, but never touch,
> feet, but never walk,
> and not a sound from their throats.
> Their makers will end up like them,
> and so will anyone who relies on them."
>
> (Ps 115:2-8)

The issue that confronts us today is not whether technology is good or bad. It is, after all, a human tool that we can use creatively or destructively. The question is one of *how*—how we choose to look

at our world, and how we choose to use our tools.
Do we have computers or do they have us? Will we
use our instruments of observation to develop the
human spirit, or will we dull our awareness of
beauty and lose our sensitivity to God? These are
some of the implications of *seeing* today.

"Seeing—we might say that the whole of life lies
in that verb." This statement of Teilhard de
Chardin underscores the urgency of the task with
which Jeremiah began his prophetic ministry. The
prophet must purify the manner in which he sees.
It is not so much the quantity and variety of
objects that we see, but the inner quality of our
hearts that matters.

It is purifying and painful to view the world with
a clean heart. The paradox and ambiguity of our
lives make it difficult to gain the perspective we
need to "interpret the times." Our horizons are
limited, and there are few clearings in the forest.
We speak today of a lack of leadership. Perhaps
we are giving expression to our inability to see
well. We find it difficult to develop the sensitivity
to life that will help us create a vision for our time.

There is a still deeper problem with the call to
see clearly. Beneath our limitations there are
fears and prejudices. Often we *cannot* see well.
But sometimes we *refuse* to see. The refusal to see
is another word for sin. Jesus tells us that we
judge ourselves by our refusal to look at the light.
"On these grounds is sentence pronounced: that
though the light has come into the world, men have
shown they prefer darkness to the light because

their deeds were evil. And indeed, everybody who
does wrong hates the light and avoids it, for fear
his actions should be exposed; but the man who
lives by the truth comes out into the light, so that it
may be plainly seen that what he does is done in
God" (Jn 3:18-21).

When Jesus cures a blind man, the Pharisees
deny that the power and love of God are at work.
They refuse to see. In contrast to the man born
blind who gains sight through faith, the Pharisees
are born physically integral but choose spiritual
blindness (Jn 9:41). There is a dimension of the
Pharisee in all of us. When we are children we are
afraid of the dark. As we grow toward adulthood,
as we make mistakes and become aware of our
sins and failures, we sometimes seek the darkness. We are afraid of the light for it reveals to us
the truth about ourselves and about life. The light
calls us to see clearly and to change radically.

In our age we are challenged, as was Jeremiah,
to look intently at ourselves and at our world. This
is a summons to move beyond the collection of data
to the vision of faith. It is not enough to know the
facts. It is not even enough to be right. We must
begin to see with the eyes of God himself.

Watching

The biblical term for this deeper form of seeing
is "watching." Watching is the vigilant awareness
of a person of faith. It is rooted in the dependency
of trust, in the personal covenant of love between
the believer and the Lord. "I wait for Yahweh,"

the psalmist prays in the night, "my soul waits for
him, I rely on his promise, my soul relies on the
Lord more than a watchman on the coming of
dawn" (Ps 130:5-6).

The psalmist provides us with an important clue
regarding the origin of the theme of watchfulness
in scripture. It is more than a religious stance. It is
rooted in a community responsibility that existed
among all ancient peoples. Watching was not a
leisure pastime, but an integral part of community
survival and growth. Because they possessed none
of our sophisticated warning devices, because
they were without radar and automatic alarm
systems, the ancient peoples depended on human
vigilance for their security. The sentinel is the
"lookout" for the entire community. He keeps
watch in the night for impending signs of danger.
He scans the horizon for significant changes in the
landscape.

We cannot fully comprehend the biblical experience of watching without placing it in this
practical context of community security. The
watchman is a minister to the life and safety of his
people. When he peers into the midnight darkness
at the edge of the camp or city he knows that the
well-being of his people rests on the quality of his
wakefulness. There is more at stake than gather-
ing information or recording facts. Watchfulness
is characterized by active waiting, by a straining
beyond self to discover the slightest movement in
the surroundings. Watching calls for more than
looking with our eyes—it is the vigilance of the

total person that is needed. More than anything else, watching demands that inner sense whereby we intuit a mood or perceive when danger is present.

In the Old Testament God reveals himself as the watchman for his people. "Near my house I will take my stand," he says through the prophet Zechariah, "like a watchman on guard against prowlers" (Zc 9:8). The shepherd image, so familiar to the people of the ancient mideast, also contains the theme of vigilance. Yahweh, the Shepherd of Israel, keeps watch for his people during the long desert nights and leads them to the new pastures of the promised land.

Jesus, too, keeps vigil. He spends the night in communion with his Father. Jesus is the sentinel of humanity. He waits for the hour of his own self-giving. He challenges those who follow him to look around and to be aware. "Be cunning as serpents," he reminds them, "and yet harmless as doves" (Mt 10:16).

Sin is the sleep of death which has descended upon the earth. The world is dominated by the powers of darkness. The call of faith is to live in the darkness without becoming part of it. When Jesus tells his disciples about the final days, he is particularly insistent that they be alert to the signs of his nearness. "Watch then, for you do not know on what day your master will come" (Mt 24:42).

Inner vigilance is necessary because the coming of the Lord will be unexpected, like a thief in the night or like the return of the master in the late

hours without warning to his servants. The most
subtle and the most dangerous temptation is to
give in to the night, to fall asleep and allow the
darkness to rule us. To watch is to fight torpor and
the dulling of our vision. "Watch and pray," Jesus
tells his disciples in the garden, "so that you do
not fall into temptation" (Mt 26:41). Jesus keeps
vigil during the final night of his struggle. Even
when those closest to him have fallen asleep, he
watches in agony and desolation. In him will be
fulfilled the watchman's longing for dawn. The
vigilance of Jesus breaks forth in the dawn of
resurrection.

St. Paul encountered this risen Lord on the road
to Damascus. He understood from personal experience the need to be watchful. It is not surprising to find his reminder to the Thessalonians:
"We are not part of the darkness or of the night.
So let us not sleep as other men, but let us rather
watch and be sober" (I Th 5:5).

The author of the book of Revelation pictures
the community of believers watching for the coming of the Lord with their best clothes, ready for
the final procession into the new Jerusalem
(Rv 16:15). There, reunited with the Risen Lord,
they will watch in joy before the throne of the
Father. "And there will be no night there"
(Rv 21:26).

For a Christian, therefore, watching is more
than wrestling with the night or being vigilant for
the presence of evil. The Christian is alert to life—
to the fulfillment that is already unfolding at the

edges of the world and in the hearts of people. Watching is another word for waiting in hope. It is conditioned by the fact that a decisive breakthrough has occurred in the night of human existence. We are not "waiting for Godot." We are not looking for an absentee landlord who will never come. In the vigilance of Jesus in the garden and on the cross, the Spirit breaks into human history. The task of the Christian watchman is to be alert to his coming and to welcome the kingdom. "How happy are your eyes because they see, your ears because they hear! I tell you solemnly, many prophets and holy men longed to see what you see, and never saw it; to hear what you hear and never heard it" (Mt 13:16-17).

What can we learn about seeing from these scriptural examples? What does the Word of God tell us about watchfulness?

We can learn that seeing is more than observing. We can grow in the awareness that watching is, first of all, an inner attitude of readiness. It is not a state of passive consciousness but the alert energy of the whole person. The watchful Christian is like the bud of the almond tree, straining toward light and life. Watchfulness is the awakened heart, the vigilant spirit. To see is to look beneath the surface toward the depth; to move beyond isolated facts to discover the presence of the Spirit, the pattern of God's coming in every moment.

There is another difference between watching

in faith and observing with detachment. It is related to the personal nature of the vigil. Prophetic vigilance summons us to go beyond scientific competence to community service and ministry.

Prophets: Watchmen of the Lord

In the Old Testament the task of being attentive to the deeper meaning of events and experience was the responsibility of a particular group in the community. This group was referred to as prophets—those who were called by God to speak for him to the entire assembly. Prophets are the watchmen of the people, the sentinels of the Spirit. The prophet stands at the watchtower of history, at the leading edge of community awareness, where he scans the horizon and listens to the winds of change. Like the Watchful Tree, the prophet strains toward the appearance of new life. He watches for the signs of God's presence in history.

Perhaps no figure in biblical literature is more misunderstood than that of the prophet. We are most familiar with the prophet in his role of seer and visionary. We often picture him as one who is concerned with the future. In doing so, we misinterpret the focus of his vision. The prophetic personality may conjure up images of crystal balls and unusual psychic powers, but this is an inadequate and even superstitious view of his mission. The primary responsibility of the prophet is that of being attuned to the present, for only in the present moment can one discover both the burden and the possibility of the future.

The prophet is a seer, but his charism and his call is to see the hidden meaning of the present moment. By becoming aware of the deeper significance of his own feelings and the currents of history, the prophet participates in shaping a vision for the future. The prophet is the watchman of God's Word, not his own word, nor the word of the current opinion polls. The question that echoes in his heart is this one: What do you *see*? What do you see now . . .?

Reading the Signs of the Times

In prophetic literature there is a phrase that characterizes this mission to understand the present more deeply. It is called "reading the signs of the times." This description contains all the significant elements of the prophet's call: (1) to reflect on the meaning of one's own life; (2) to be sensitive to the presence of God in the world; (3) to interpret the flow of history in the light of God's Word.

The question of who exercises the prophetic task was a source of tension in the Old Testament. The authentic prophets see the task of vigilance more and more as a communal one. When an argument arises regarding the credentials of prophecy and who has the right to exercise it, Moses intervenes. He says to those who are arguing among themselves: "If only the whole people of

Yahweh were prophets, and Yahweh gave his Spirit to them all" (Nb 11:29). The prophet Joel also spoke of the era when all people would be filled with the Spirit of God and would participate in the mission of reading the signs of the times. "After this I will pour out my spirit on all mankind. Your sons and daughters shall prophesy, your old men shall dream dreams, and your young men see visions. Even on the slaves, men and women, will I pour out my spirit in those days" (Jl 3:1-2).

Joel's prophecy is fulfilled in the experience of Pentecost when the new Israel is born. All Christians are filled with the Spirit and exercise the role of vigilance in the world.

The prophetic task of watchfulness became a significant theme in the Second Vatican Council. "Reading the signs of the times" was a favorite phrase of Pope John XXIII in his encyclical, *Peace on Earth*. When it was introduced into the discussions of the Second Vatican Council many of the Council fathers found it unfamiliar and confusing. It was, nevertheless, an important regrounding of the Church in the biblical tradition. One of the Council's most significant documents, *Gaudium et Spes*, opens with this theme: "To carry out such a task [serving the world in love], the church has always had the duty of scrutinizing the signs of the times and of interpreting them in the light of the gospel" (*Gaudium et Spes*, 4).

What is involved in the contemporary task of reading the signs of our times? Perhaps we can best answer this question by describing what it does not mean. First, reading the signs of the times is not the same as "knowing the facts." The quest of the human heart for meaning obviously has something to do with the actual events and discoveries, the scientific data and the research which influence our decisions and our planning. The Christian watchman must deal with this flood of events and information. But we cannot afford to mistake facts for truth. The signs of the times are not contained in government statistics nor in the latest economic index. The signs of the times are expressed in the deeper currents of struggle and of awareness where the human heart seeks to break through the facts to touch life.

Secondly, reading the signs of the times is not the same as "following the fads." The prophet does not guide his life by the latest opinion polls or by current social movements. We are not called to grasp at what is merely popular or convenient or politically expedient. Often the responsibility of being watchful will leave us on what appears to be the edges of society. The prophet is not called to popularity, but rather to discern the presence of the Spirit in history. St. Paul gives us this advice: "Do not conform yourselves to this age but be transformed by the renewal of your mind" (Ep 5:16).

The Christian prophet is not called to popularity, but to the lonely task of watching in the night. He must learn to look deeper than the microscope and farther than the telescope. Christian vigilance leads us beyond advertising and public relations to the real needs of people. It puts us into touch with loneliness and with the ache of the heart for meaning. These currents of life often hide behind popular trends. They are discovered behind social masks and beyond the fashions of the day.

What are the signs of the times? They are the outer circumstances of history which are capable of expressing God's Word and which are open to being shaped by his Spirit. The signs of the times are the moods of our inner weather. Jesus condemned his contemporaries because they were familiar with the signs of outer weather but blind to the weather of the heart. A prophet is a meteorologist of the spirit. He knows when there is a storm rising; he senses when it is dawn, and where to look for the quiet of peace. This is because the signs are unique to each age. They are not only signs, they are signs of *these times*.

Christian vigilance requires that we know "what time it is." Time, in the biblical sense, is more than the simple measurement of movement from moment to moment. Time is the unfolding of salvation history. To tell time as a Christian is to be sensitive to the opportune moment—that decisive coming together of events and possibilities that creates a breakthrough of the Spirit. This is what Jesus refers to as his "hour" and what Paul describes as the "kairos"—the *now* of greatest possibility and creativity.

The kingdom is coming into the world. At certain moments it has the possibility of a real breakthrough. Jesus encourages us to know when

those moments are present: "Have you not got a
saying: 'Four months and then the harvest?' Well,
I tell you: Look around you, look at the fields;
already they are white, ready for harvest! Already the reaper is being paid his wages, already
he is bringing in the grain for eternal life"
(Jn 4:35). Jesus weeps over his city, Jerusalem,
because the people did not know the time of the
Lord's visitation. They did not understand the
things that would have brought them peace. They
were not watching for the Lord's coming.

Watching: A Personal Task

The personal call to vigilance is an experience
of both prayer and poetry. It emerges in the attentive stance of faith and it is expressed in the
language of the imagination. Herbert Read describes the artist as "the antenna of society,"
because the artist intuits those experiences for
which society cannot yet find words or symbols.
On the level of imagination the artist is already
creating the future. The same is true of the
prophet. As the "antenna of the Spirit" the Christian prophet is attuned to the deeper movement of
life. Through the watchfulness of prayer he
creates an openness within which the Spirit can
renew the earth. To watch is to create a "beachhead" for the kingdom, a space for the new
creation.

What do you *see?* This is the urgent question
which God places before us today. We cannot
read the signs around us unless we know the

moments of our own lives. We cannot be sentinels of the Spirit in the world if we do not wait through the long watches of our own night. Watching begins with self. And there the night is longest. When we are vigilant toward our own lives it is more than an act of watching, it is an experience of wrestling. Like the patriarch, Jacob, we wrestle with God in the night of our growth. Before we can read the signs of the times, we ourselves must be tested. We must be "read" by the Spirit.

Isaiah could not speak to his age until his lips were purified by the burning coals. Jeremiah groped toward vision through the night of depression and personal uncertainty. His call led him to the edge of despair as often as it led him to understanding. Ezechiel could not encourage the exiles until he had eaten the scroll of the lamentations. Before he could speak of hope he had to experience fully the devastation of his people and of his age.

What is significant in all of these examples is that the outer experience of life must be faced inwardly. Watching as a prophet begins with inward wrestling. The key to vision in the world lies in the dark terrain of the heart. The Word of God must get inside us where, as the author of Hebrews puts it, "it cuts like any double-edged sword but more finely: it can slip through the place where the soul is divided from the spirit, or joints from the marrow; it can judge the secret emotions and thoughts" (Heb 4:12). Only when we have watched at the outposts of our own lives can we hear the cries of the prisoners. Only then will we begin to see with eyes of fire.

One day Francis of Assisi stood before the Watchful Tree. He said: "Speak to me of God." And the almond tree blossomed.

Like Francis we stand before the world with a sense of expectancy. We see that it is broken and divided. We see that it is desperate for a sign of hope. We hesitate, and then form the words, if not with our lips, then in our hearts. We say: Speak to me of God.

In the morning there are blossoms.

Chapter Two

WITHOUT A VISION THE PEOPLE PERISH

The Crisis in Spirituality

"The human heart can go the lengths of God.
Dark and cold we may be, but this
Is no winter now. The frozen misery
Of centuries breaks, cracks, begins to move;
The thunder is the thunder of the floes,
The thaw, the flood, the upstart Spring.
Thank God our time is now when wrong
Comes up to face us everywhere,
Never to leave us till we take
The longest stride of soul man ever took.
Affairs are now soul size,
The enterprise
Is exploration into God."

—Christopher Fry
A Sleep of Prisoners

Enough Light To See

One day an old Rabbi asked his followers this question: "How do you know when there is enough light to see?"

One of his disciples answered, "There is enough light to see when you can see the current of the river move through the morning mist."

"No," replied the Rabbi, "That is not enough light."

33

A second disciple replied, "There is enough light to see when you can tell an oak tree from a sycamore."

"No," replied the Rabbi, "that is not enough light."

A third disciple said, "There is enough light to see when you can distinguish the young lambs from the goats as they romp in the morning light."

"No," replied the Rabbi, "that is still not enough light."

Then his followers looked at the Rabbi and were silent.

Finally the old master raised his eyes and spoke with deliberation. "There is enough light to see," he said, "when you can look into the eyes of another person and understand that he or she is your brother or your sister."[1]

Finding enough light to see is the prophetic task of every Christian in our time. The story of the Rabbi illustrates the levels of watchfulness which were discussed in the first chapter. He challenges his followers to seek a deeper and more personal way of viewing life. He invites them to read the signs of the times from the vantage point of trust. The light which we need to see is more than common sense or scientific insight. It is the light of faith. It is an inward attentiveness which is ultimately rooted in love. There is enough light to see when we view the world with the same compassion with which we look into the eyes of those we love.

The Signs of Our Times

If we look with this kind of sensitivity, what will the times reveal to us? If we are watchful with the eyes of faith, what will we see? What *are* the signs of our times?

The events and trends of every age are multiple and diverse. The political and social conditions of our time are not only complex, they are also changing with a rapidity unparalleled in history. "Future shock," writes Alvin Toffler, "is the premature arrival of the future." Many of us are experiencing this kind of shock. The technological explosion continues to change our style of life at an ever-increasing rate. We are plunging ahead so rapidly that we easily lose contact with the present moment. In Marshall McLuhan's phrase, we find ourselves looking at the present "through a rear-view mirror." One of the signs of our times is the experience of change, rapid and all-pervasive change.

But there is more at stake than the rapidity with which change is taking place. There is also the question of the quality and the nature of that change. The events and scientific breakthroughs affect not only the outer circumstances of our lives, but also the inner world of our awareness and of our personal sense of meaning. They shape our values and our vision, our way of responding to life. "Today the human race is passing through a new stage of its history . . . we can already speak of a true social and cultural transformation, one which has repercussions on man's religious life as well" (Gaudium et Spes, 4). These are the words in which the fathers of the Second Vatican Council describe the significance of change in our century.

The second major sign of our times is the experience of crisis which follows in the wake of change. Social and cultural transformation cannot take place without a major upheaval in human life. Vatican II describes this upheaval as "a crisis of growth" (Gaudium et Spes, 4). Others do not view the crisis with the same hopefulness. They look upon the sweeping tide of change with alarm rather than optimism. In the face of crumbling political and social structures many people are becoming cynical and disillusioned. They fear that the technological revolution is simply the last bright glow of a star which is about to fade. In the universities, there are discussions about the decline and fall of western civilization. At conferences and cocktail parties, concerned people raise questions regarding the survival of the human race and the future of our planet.

How does the Christian watchman understand the significance of this crisis? As sentinels of the Spirit what do we see?

There are different ways of interpreting the crisis which rapid change has brought about in our lives. It might be helpful to summarize them briefly here.

A Crisis of Technology

There are some in our society who believe that we are experiencing a technological crisis. Our scientific know-how has developed so rapidly that it has created unforeseen side effects in our environment and in the quality of our life. These problems can be remedied by further research and development. Since technology created the problems, technology can also solve them. The crisis we face is simply one of know-how. To meet the crisis it is necessary to raise more funds for research and to spend more money on scientific development.

This point of view holds that the environmental crisis does not demand a critical re-evaluation of our life style, nor does it require us to examine the extent to which industry is exploiting our natural resources. It simply calls for more technological breakthroughs. It invites us to explore ways in which we might apply scientific research to the control and interpretation of human behavior.

A Crisis of Culture

A second group in our society believes that there is more at stake than scientific development. The technological crisis is, in their opinion, only a symptom of a more fundamental cultural upheaval. The key to the crisis is to be found beneath the surface of science at the level of culture. In

their view the nature of social behavior is under-
going a revolution. The crisis is linked with the
question of whether or not the human species can
adapt to new emotional and psychic pressures. It
is also related to the challenge of developing new
family and societal structures—structures which
will insure maximum freedom and growth for the
individual.

A Crisis of Spirituality

There are aspects of truth in both of the above
interpretations. Some of the challenges that we
face are related to the creative development and
use of technology. Others are related to more
complex factors that affect our personal identity
and our social relationships.

These approaches have one thing in common—
they interpret the signs of our times primarily in
terms of *external* circumstances. They understand
change as something that happens to us from the
outside. As a result, they look to external forces—
scientific research or social adaptation—to resolve the crisis.

For a Christian, neither of these approaches is
sufficient. In order to read the signs of the times
we must look more deeply. We must look with the
eyes of faith.

First of all, as Christians, we approach the
experience of crisis with an attitude of hope. We
believe that human life is more than problem-
solving or cultural adaptation. It is responding to
the presence of God in history. In any crisis we see

promise as well as pain. A crisis is a call to growth, and growth, like change of any kind, is an experience of conflict and tension. Change is a universal law. It continues to take place in our lives and in our world whether we fear it and resist it, or whether we accept it and creatively shape it.

The ancient philosopher Heraclitus once said, "You never put your foot into the same river twice." Time is the river and its current calls us to be pilgrims. We fear change and cling to the security of what we know, even when it is an experience of stagnation.

We generally assume that crisis is another word for collapse. Many crises have the outward appearance of disintegration, but they also contain within them the possibility of growth. In his book *Reveille for Radicals,* Saul Alinsky points out that the Chinese write the word "crisis" with two characters. One of the characters symbolizes *danger;* the other means *opportunity.* A crisis is a dangerous opportunity.[2] Unfortunately, we spend so much of our energy trying to escape from the danger that we often miss the opportunity.

Krisis, the Greek word, means to cut or to judge. At a time of crisis we are confronted with choices. We cannot remain passive. We must act. It is a moment of separation and struggle, a tearing apart of the energies of growth from the atrophied remains of the past. At times of crisis we walk at the cutting edges of our lives.

Secondly, we find that the scientific and cultural interpretations are lacking in depth. Neither goes far enough. Neither touches the inner world where every crisis must ultimately be resolved. Both interpretations stop short of the world of the Spirit where we seek for meaning and hunger for God. The forms which the contemporary crisis take in technology and culture are really only outward manifestations of this deeper struggle.

Theodore Roszak describes this inner crisis in this way: "We can now recognize that the fate of the soul is the fate of the social order; that if the spirit within us withers, so too will all the world we build about us. Literally so. What after all, is the ecological crisis that now captures so much belated attention but the inevitable extroversion of a blighted psyche? Like inside, like outside. In the eleventh hour, the very physical environment suddenly looms up before us as the outward mirror of our inner condition."[3]

This is not a new insight, but it is a very significant one. It simply states in contemporary terms what Jesus tells his followers: "What goes into the mouth does not make a man unclean; it is what comes out of the mouth that makes him unclean" (Mt 15:11). In this passage Jesus re-affirms the priority of inner attitudes over their external manifestations. The struggle for significance is won or lost in this inner world. This is the arena where we must look to understand today's crisis. The deepest quest of our hearts is the search for God. The most critical challenge is the invitation to believe. It is not the technological know-how that we lack, nor the academic re-

sources to interpret the emerging shape of culture. What we lack is a sense of personal *meaning*, an inner purpose, a reason to go on. "Without
a vision the people perish," writes the author of
Proverbs (cf. Pr 11:14).

As Christian watchmen we look with vigilant
awareness into the turmoil around us. We look
past peripheral explanations to find the pulse of
the Spirit. We recognize the dangers but we
continue to search for the opportunities. We see
beyond the crisis of technology and culture to the
world of the spirit, where the human heart seeks
for God. On this level the crisis calls for more than
a solution. It calls for growth. It calls us to journey
through danger toward the promise of new life. It
is a time when we experience the mystery and the
ambiguity of human life. We find ourselves listen-
ing again to the words of Jesus. They are alive
with new meaning: "Unless a wheat grain falls on
the ground and dies, it remains only a single grain;
but if it dies, it yields a rich harvest" (Jn 12:24).
The dangerous opportunities of life are translated
in scriptural language as the journey through
death to new life.

Our scientists search for improved technology.
The philosophers and historians continue to study
the developments of culture. And in the watchfulness of faith we scan the skies of the heart. The
cutting edge of life is in the world of the spirit. The
turning point of history is at the center of the self.
It is faith itself that is at stake. The crisis of our
age is beyond computers and systems analysts. It
is deeper than popular psychology and new

theories of culture. It is, in a word, a crisis of
spirituality.

The Search For A Vision

The first indications of this crisis came in the
late 50s and the early 60s. During the "Fabulous
Fifties" the United States experienced a continuous wave of technological growth. The
economy held strong; the universities were
crowded; the churches flourished. Optimism ran
high.

But all was not well. The restlessness of the
early 60s gave rise to the civil rights movement
and to student unrest on university and college
campuses. As the nation sank deeper into the
quagmire of Southeast Asia, the conflict at home
escalated. There were the assassinations, the long
hot summers of racial violence, the generation
gap. Theologians spoke of the death of God. Everywhere were signs of crumbling trust and hope.
The young experimented with drugs. The crime
rate rose. Political corruption increased. The
environment reflected outwardly the brokenness
and disillusionment that many people felt inwardly. We began to speak with concern about
the quality of life. We knew, without saying it, that
we were speaking about more than clean air and
water.

At the time, most of us interpreted the 60s as a
decade of political and social unrest. It was an
era, we thought, when the impact of the technological revolution was felt in the collective psyche
of the nation and of the world.

It was this, but it was much more. It is a serious mistake to read the signs of any time in purely political or social terms. Beneath the political protest there was a cry for human meaning. Beneath the social unrest there were deeper hungers stirring. People went into the streets to express political dissent. They walked home questioning the meaning of their lives and the purpose of human freedom. In the face of conflict and violence the human spirit was driven back to fundamental issues. The real struggle was not in the streets nor on college campuses, but in the inner life of a whole generation of people. "It is not the barricades I fear," said a student in Paris, "but the burning bush."

Without a vision the people perish. We began to grope for a vision.

A glimpse of that vision came to us from the dark side of the moon. We watched in wonderment as technology lifted history into outer space. Through the miracle of television we made the journey with the astronauts. As we came around the other side of the earth's satellite we discovered something far more important than moon rocks. We discovered ourselves looking into a technological mirror. There, on the horizon of the moon, we saw ourselves on television. For the first time in history, human beings saw an earthrise. In that moment a new consciousness was born. We became aware of how beautiful and bright, and yet how small and fragile is our earth. We were in awe of our powers. We were humbled by our responsibility. The wide, wide world became spaceship earth. Our planet became a global village.

We went to the moon, but we rediscovered the earth. We went in search of scientific data. We returned with a few rocks and a new understanding of ourselves. The moon trip became a journey of the spirit. Technology had succeeded. It had succeeded so well that it forced us to confront the mystery of our fears and our possibilities. We touched the taproot of the human condition. We encountered the dark nobility and uncertainty of living on this planet. From the dark side of the moon we began to find enough light to see. . . .

The hunger for inward meaning had begun even before we explored outer space. We groped our way through the sounds and rhythms of change and then turned to find our souls. The Beatles, the folk heroes of the 60s, turned from rock music to drugs, from drugs to oriental meditation, and finally to silence. Their story is not an isolated one. It reflects a general turning inward in search of identity and purpose, a quest for values and a sense of direction. In an age of upheaval, we turned to rediscover our roots and to touch life.

We bought campers and backpacking equipment. We went in search of the earth. We read Carl Rogers and joined encounter groups. We attended sessions on communication and explored group dynamics. We wanted to re-win the broken bonds of relationships and touch the uniqueness of our feelings. We dabbled in the occult and experimented with altered states of consciousness. We studied oriental philosophy and practiced yoga.

We sang with the flower children and prayed with the Jesus freaks. We explored transcendental meditation and ate natural foods. We put up banners and kept journals. And now, like the Beatles, we are silent.

"Now that my ladder's gone," writes Yeats, "I must lie down where all ladders start, in the foul rag-and-bone shop of the heart."

Our ladder is gone. We've walked in the streets and come home. We've gone to the moon and returned to the earth. The social problems are not solved and the political tensions go on. The crisis is not over. It has only moved to the source of all outward change—the inner world of human search. We now have enough light to see. We know now that we must begin where all ladders start—in the foul rag-and-bone shop of the heart.

The Search For A Spirituality

The crisis of our age has brought us back to our inner selves, but it has not necessarily brought us back to faith. It has confronted us with the world of the spirit but it has not given us a spirituality. It has brought us into touch with our hunger for transcendence but it has not given us the presence of God.

The search for God eventually leads us back to the Church. To speak of spirituality we must speak of the experience of the community of faith. What effect has the crisis of change had on the Church? What are the signs of the times within the Christian Community?

In answering this we can only begin by acknowledging that, until recently, the Church has resisted change. The Church has attempted to preserve its role as a stable presence in a rapidly changing world. As the tempo of change continued to pick up, many Catholics depended upon the Church to remain the secure reference point in their lives.

Dependence on the Church for this kind of security began to change with Pope John XXIII and the Second Vatican Council. We were invited to become a pilgrim people. We sought to re-win our identity as the people of God. In the intervening years we have learned that to be called "the people of God" is more than a change in words. It defines our mission and the way in which we live our lives. The Church is not called to live at the sidelines of history. Jesus did not tell his followers to live on the shore. He invited them to cast out into the deep. He calls us to follow him into the world. The Word became flesh and lives among us. Today the Church is following the Lord back into the marketplace of life. We pitch our tents with the other pilgrims. In the marketplace we join our brothers and sisters in looking for a vision. We too are experiencing a crisis of spirituality.

Pope John called the council to renew the inner life of God's people. It was his hope that the Church might, in turn, minister to the needs of the world, especially the poor and the oppressed, the outcasts and the brokenhearted.

In the years immediately following the Council it appeared that we had forgotten the central call to *inner* renewal. The new vision of the Church

stirred enthusiasm for reform on all levels. At
first, it seemed as though we were identifying
reform with external reorganization. We con-
centrated our efforts on reshaping the forms of
worship and the structures of the Church. We
revised the language and the rites of the liturgy.
We struggled to move the Church from an au-
thoritarian model to a collegial community in
which there is shared responsibility and mutual
dialogue. All of this was necessary, even when it
created conflict and division within the Church.
But in the process we frequently forgot the call to
inward renewal.

We now have the structures necessary for
renewal. The liturgical and sacramental rites
have been revised. The Church is more collegial in
its makeup and in its organization. The channels
are available for dialogue. The challenge facing us
now is that of putting flesh on the structures. Just
as it is a mistake to interpret the crisis in society
as purely political or social, so it is also inadequate to view the crisis in the Church as
though it were only a question of new rites or
changing structures. The challenge is deeper than
that. We are hungry for God. We are searching
for faith. We are groping for a vision that will
make the structures come alive and enable the
Church to be a leaven in today's world.

The most significant sign of the times in the
Church today is the renewed hunger for spirituality. It is a restlessness for a more intense life of
prayer. It is the budding of a spirit of contemplation. The Church is in search of its soul.

The Meaning of Spirituality

The crisis of our age is a call to explore the world of the spirit. This, in turn, raises another question. What is the meaning of *spirituality*? It is a term that is easily misunderstood in the history of the Church. For centuries we have wrestled with the temptation to separate the soul from the body, the life of the spirit from the everyday world of human experience. The most subtle but persistent heresy in Christianity has not been the denial of Christ's divinity, but the refusal to accept his humanity. It is not only the humanity of Jesus that is at stake; it is the acceptance of the human condition in each of our lives. Spirituality is not a separate compartment of the self that stands apart from the flow of life. It is not a list of rules or a series of disciplinary regulations. It does not refer to unusual religious behavior. It is not limited to an esoteric group called "saints". Spirituality is not an escape clause or a religious tranquilizer. It is a vision which enables us to accept our lives as human.

In simplest terms, spirituality is the life of the spirit—the creative presence of God's Spirit as he moves over the chaotic waters of the world and as he searches out the loneliness of our hearts. Spirituality is the vision. It is the motivating energy that gives us a reason for life and the creative power which enables us to live it.

The Hebrews called it "Torah"—the Law. In its original context the Torah referred to the total way of life for a follower of Yahweh. It referred to the life of worship, work, family relationships, social responsibilities, and the basic values of life. Torah implies the total response of the believer to Yahweh. It is the covenant as it is enfleshed in the lives of individuals. It is only later that the Pharisees reduced the Torah to a rigid set of rules. Jesus condemned this over-zealous desire to turn the personal covenant of love into a sterile observance of regulations. "I have not come to abolish the Torah," he said, "but to bring it to fulfillment." It was not Jesus' intention to destroy the religious vision of his ancestors. He came to perfect and to complete the spirituality of the Old Testament. He came to return the Torah to its original covenantal roots, and, through his death and resurrection, to transform it into a new way of life. Christian spirituality is a flowering of the faith of Abraham in the person of Jesus and in his Body, the Church.

The Chinese use the word *Tao*—the Way. The Tao includes more than methods of meditation or principles for self-discipline. Tao is the flow and process of inner growth. It is the total response of a person who seeks for enlightenment and liberation. The Tao is also a spirituality, a vision of the ultimate meaning of human life.

Today we might use the term "life-style" to describe what we mean by spirituality. Life style refers to the personal vision we have of ourselves and of our values. It is the way we define our lives. It encompasses the conscious, chosen values which motivate our growth and which find expression in the circumstances of our living. Our life style is more than the clothes we wear or the consumer goods that surround our lives. It is the values out of which we choose the direction of our personal existence. Life style is an expression of spirituality.

Jesus did not explicitly use the term spirituality. He spoke of the kingdom of the Father that is within us. He challenged his followers to be converted in their fundamental stance toward life. He described the qualities of the heart that are necessary for someone to be born into everlasting life. He stressed the priority of inner attitudes over outward observance. He spoke of the totality with which we must respond to the Father. He challenged his followers to take up their cross daily to follow him.

Taken separately, Jesus' admonitions are like strands of spirituality. Taken together, they form an integral vision of Christian life. There is one passage in particular which expresses Jesus' attitude toward spirituality. It is found in Luke's gospel as part of the parable of the lamp. "The lamp of your body is your eye. When your eye is sound, your whole body too is filled with light; but when it is diseased your body too will be all darkness. If, therefore, your whole body is filled with light, and no trace of darkness, it will be light entirely, as when the lamp shines on you with its rays" (Lk 11:34-36).

Jesus uses the eye as a symbol of spiritual vision. If we substitute the word "life" for the word "body" in this passage, and the word "spirituality" for the word "eye," we would have a summary of the gospel's attitude toward the place of spirituality in our lives. When your spirituality is sound, your whole life, too, is filled with light; but when it is diseased your life too will be all darkness. See to it then that the light inside you is not darkness. If, therefore, your whole life is filled with light, and no trace of darkness, it will be light entirely, as when the lamp shines on you with its rays.

All around us there are signs that the hunger for spiritual growth is increasing. Serious Christians want to do more than keep the laws of the Church or practice their religion in a narrow sense. They want to deepen their relationship with the Father and share the experience of community with their fellow Christians. They want to be a vital part of the Church's mission to society. This renewal of interest in spirituality is taking place at different levels, but it is found with special enthusiasm among small, local communities. It is emerging in prayer groups, in religious orders, in priest support groups, in small communities concerned for justice and peace, in cursillos and in charismatic communities, in directed retreats and marriage encounters, and in programs of spiritual renewal in parishes.

Ultimately, of course, growth in spirituality begins with individuals and their faith response. A shared vision of life is only as vibrant as the commitment and participation of individual Christians. The worship of the Church shapes and is shaped by the prayer life of its members. There is

Novitiate Library

strong evidence that the Spirit is at work in individual lives. The desire to live the gospel with renewed intensity is spreading. The crisis in the Church has given us enough light to see what really matters. The search for spirituality is the most important sign of our times.

Recently a devastating earthquake left the people of Guatemala stunned by death and destruction. Many of them had nothing left in worldly terms. There seemed to be no way to rebuild. But in the midst of the ruins they mobilized their hope and their efforts. On buses and street cars, in restaurants, on collapsed buildings and in mountain villages there were signs that announced: *Guatemala esta en pied!*—"Guatemala is on its feet!"

The people of Guatemala have given us an important message. We have not experienced the physical devastation that swept through their land, but we have felt the shock waves of change. We have not had to rebuild entire villages and towns, but we have experienced an upheaval in the structures of our society and of our Church. We have experienced an earthquake of spirituality. There is a sense of confusion and disillusionment. All around us we see the ruins of the past. The temptation to despair or to cynicism is strong. But in the midst of the crisis there are signs of hope. The Spirit is moving in our world. We have become pilgrims again. Like Guatemala, we are on our feet.

Chapter Three

COME BACK TO ME

Rediscovering Our Roots

"I am a pilgrim of the future on
my way back from a journey made
entirely in the past."
—Teilhard de Chardin,
China, 1923

On the side streets of San Salvador there are
signs that read: "Vote For The New Man. Vote
Marxist!" It was not the political party that caught
my attention as much as the promise of a new
humanity. At first glance it appeared to be one
more instance of political propaganda. But beneath the smeared paint and the crude lettering I
sensed more than rhetoric. The search for a new
vision of humanity is not limited to the Marxists. It
is an unspoken hunger in all of us. Today we are
restless for a revolution that will go beyond
political ideology and economic theory. We are
seeking for a new model of the self, a new way of
experiencing our humanity.

Somewhere in the coffee fields of El Salvador
there is a new man. He doesn't fit the usual
description of a revolutionary. He is neither
Marxist nor capitalist. He is not well-educated
nor skilled in technology. His occupation does not
qualify him for regular promotions or for fringe
benefits. But there is one gift that he does have.

He is close to the earth. He is a *campesino*—a peasant farmer who struggles to support his family by cultivating someone else's land in the mountains of Central America. He works the earth, but he also burns with the desire to create a new humanity. His name is Danilo. He has reason to be on fire. Danilo is a Christian.

I listened to Danilo one evening as he preached a homily at a prayer service. About thirty other *campesinos*, men and women, sat on benches in the open air pavillion which served as chapel and classroom. It was one of many sessions held at a center for Christian formation. In this setting hundreds of lay leaders have participated in courses on the Christian gospel and its social implications. Here they are prepared to become health promoters, community organizers, and catechists in the outlying villages.

Danilo graduated from the center as a catechist three years ago. Now he serves as a leader of prayer and ministry in his rural community. As I listened to him that warm summer evening, I could sense the stirrings of a revolution. I could see the vision of a new humanity in the making. Despite the language barrier, Danilo's message was clear. It was clear that he is a man of the earth who listens to the sounds of the Spirit. It was clear that he is a watchman for his people and for the Lord. It was clear that he reads the signs of his times with sensitivity and understanding. It was clear that he had discovered the spirituality of the gospel and that its vision permeates his life.

Still, there was something that I could not com-

prehend about Danilo. There was a quality of
dedication that went beyond vision and commitment. He possessed an energy that seemed inex-
haustible. Where did it come from? What made
him so vibrant?

The answer came in Danilo's homily. He was
speaking on the role of the Christian prophet.
After summarizing the biblical background, Danilo
shared his personal description of a prophet. "A
prophet," he said, "is someone who carries his
past experience of God into the present with such
conviction that he is able to create a vision for the
future."

That was it! Through faith, Danilo had come
into contact with the taproot of his life. He had
touched the presence of God in the Christian
tradition and in his own past with so much awareness that it had transformed his life. Danilo
carried his past experience of God into the present
with such conviction that he was able to create a
vision of the future.

Danilo might not qualify as a professional theo-
logian, but he challenged me to understand the
prophetic call of the Christian in a new way. He
also helped me to understand something very
essential in the contemporary search for spirituality. He pointed to the need we have of rediscovering our roots.

The Experience of Uprootedness

One of the signs of our time is the widespread
experience of uprootedness. We can trace the
causes of this "dis-ease" to many different

sources. It is characteristic of transition times like our own when change is so rapid that we easily lose our emotional bearings. It arises because of the increased mobility of our age. It arises because people change occupations more often. It arises when entire families move from one end of the country to the other because of the demands of industry or business. It is found among the world's refugees as they flee from war, oppression, famine, or earthquake. It is found among the affluent in the form of restlessness and in the vague realization that something is missing in their lives. It is found in the Church among Christians who feel that the renewal has passed them by without touching their lives.

Many Catholics sensed that the Church was in need of renewal, but they weren't sure about the direction the renewal should take. They did not have a clear grasp of the essentials of Christianity in contrast with those things which developed as cultural or devotional accretions. Like Danilo, the church needs to touch the taproot of the gospel.

The Pattern of Renewal

Growth in spirituality begins in an attitude of watchfulness. It continues to develop in the experience of rediscovering our roots. Danilo's reflection on the meaning of a Christian prophet reminded me of the vision of Pope John XXIII. The peasant from Bergamo had been pope for only ninety days when, on January 25, 1959, he made the first and unexpected announcement of his plan to convoke the Church's twenty-first ecumenical council. The person whom many people regarded as a transitional pope was about to lead the Church into an era of unparalleled transition. In his announcement, John singled out the personal renewal of faith as the primary goal of the Second Vatican Council. To accomplish this goal he proposed a double movement of the spirit. First, he challenged the Church to return to the essential teaching and experience of the Christian life as it is found in the gospel and in the life of the early Christian community. Secondly, he invited the Church to create new structures and forms of mission and worship which would make the gospel relevant in today's world. This rhythm of reflection and action is basic to the renewal of faith and spirituality today. Creativity demands contemplation. *Aggiornamento* is a prophetic task. It implies that we must recover the central experience of the gospel and carry it into this age with such conviction that we will create a new future.

"We live our lives forward," writes Kierkegaard, "but we understand them backward." In the past several years we have been living forward. We have plunged ahead recklessly toward a collision between the demands of technology and the limits of nature. The sounds of that collision are all around us. We hear it each time a group of citizens calls for an environmental impact study. Slowly we are learning the necessity of reflection.

Before developing new technology we are taking
time to recover our roots in the earth and to
reassess the implications of science.

The same is true in the Church. In the last
decade we have moved ahead boldly to change
structures and to revise our forms of worship. But
we too are learning the necessity of reflection.
Renewal demands rediscovery. It demands that
we, like Danilo, recover our roots.

Rediscovery vs. Nostalgia

What is involved in the act of rediscovering our
roots? This is an important question because it
can be answered in different and conflicting ways.

Rediscovering our roots is not the same as
wanting to live in the past. There are many
Catholics today who would prefer to stop living
forward altogether. They are frightened by the
demands of renewal and they want to turn back.
It is the static, hierarchical Church of the recent
past that they want to recover, not the primordial
experience of the gospel or of the early Christian
community. They have in mind a tableau from
their childhood, an image of the Church as stable,
well-ordered and at peace. This is nostalgia, not
renewal. It is escape rather than rediscovery. We
find a parallel to this attitude in the Old Testament
account of the Exodus. When God led his people
out of Egypt there was an initial burst of confidence and enthusiasm. After a long period of
slavery the people were free to rediscover the God

of their Fathers. Then came the desert. It is one
thing to escape from slavery; it is another thing to
walk into the unknown. The journey toward freedom is a long and frightening experience. The
people began to look back in regret. The author of
Exodus describes it in this way: "The whole community of the sons of Israel began to complain
against Moses and Aaron in the wilderness and
said to them, 'Why did we not die at Yahweh's
hand in the land of Egypt, when we were able to
sit down to pans of meat and could eat to our
heart's content! As it is, you have brought us to
this wilderness to starve this whole company to
death' " (Ex 16:2-3)!

In the Exodus event Yahweh called his people
back to their roots. In order for them to journey
forward to a new land they first had to recover
the desert relationship that their fathers, Abraham, Isaac and Jacob, had once had with God.
Nostalgia would have taken them back to the
secure, but oppressed life of Egypt. Renewal sum-
moned them into the wilderness to rediscover their
covenant with Yahweh and to become a new
people.

Like the Israelites we are frightened by the
desert. There are many who are tempted to nostalgia. They want to turn back. But our roots, like
those of Israel, lie deeper than the recent past
with its security. Our roots can be found only in
the wilderness.

Nietzsche once said that "the things which do

not kill us, strengthen us." This is also true of the call to follow God through the desert. By the time of the prophets, the wilderness journey had become the most cherished event in the memory of the Israelite people. The desert was another name for intimacy with God. It was the time in sacred history when the Israelites were most fully alive to his care and love for them. It was the time when they heard the call of Yahweh most clearly. The wilderness journey was Israel's central experience of faith.

During the time of the kings, Israel frequently fell back into a settled, easy religion of ritualism and outward observance. They often adopted the cultic practices of their neighbors with their emphasis on the security of nature rather than the adventure of sacred history. At these times the prophets appeared to speak God's Word to his people. The prophets came from many different classes of society. They were priests and shepherds. They were willing and unwilling. They were varied in personality and style. But beneath the human differences there was a common experience and a common mission. Their message had a similar ring to it: Come back to me! Be converted! Turn back to the covenant which I made with your ancestors in the desert. In a word, the prophets challenged the people to rediscover their roots. Invariably this was portrayed as a return to the desert experience. Hosea compares the Lord's relationship to Israel with that of a

husband who invites his wife to return to the
faithfulness and tenderness of their early love:

". . . I am going to lure her
and lead her out into the wilderness
and speak to her heart.
I am going to give her back her vineyards,
and make the Valley Achor a gateway of hope.
There she will respond to me as she did when she was
    young,
as she did when she came out of the land of Egypt.

When that day comes—it is Yahweh who speaks—
she will call me, 'My husband',
no longer will she call me, 'My Baal'.
I will take the names of the Baals off her lips,
their names shall never be uttered again.

When that day comes I will make a treaty on her behalf
    with the wild animals,
with the birds of heaven and the creeping things of
    the earth;
I will break bow, sword and battle in the country,
and make her sleep secure.
I will betroth you to myself for ever,
betroth you with integrity and justice,
with tenderness and love;
I will betroth you to myself with faithfulness,
and you will come to know Yahweh." (Ho 2:16-22)

The prophets do not invite the Israelites into a
world of nostalgia. They do not offer a world of
complacency that is free from fear or from the
tension of growth. They challenge the Israelites to
rediscover the original experience through which
they were transformed from a scattered group of

slaves into the people of God. They are calling them back to the insecurity of the wilderness. They challenge them to risk everything for God.

The prophetic call to rediscover roots is a model for our contemporary experience. The Spirit is calling the Church to rediscover its roots in the same way in which the prophets once did. The paschal journey of Jesus is to us what the exodus event was for the Israelites. The passage of Jesus through death to new life is the primordial event of Christianity. The Church refers to this new and definitive Exodus as "the Paschal Mystery." Through our participation in this mystery we receive our call as Christians and our identity as the new people of God.

Rediscovering our roots involves two related experiences. First, it calls us to conversion. This is the initial willingness to "turn around" and to open ourselves to God's presence. It also involves a willingness to turn aside from ritualism and the mere outward observance of laws. It is an invitation to stand ready for a new journey into the wilderness.

The second aspect of rediscovering our roots is what is described in scripture as *anamnesis*—"remembering." This is more than simply recalling a forgotten fact. It is not just a case of "refreshing our memory." Rembering is an encounter with God. In the act of remembering we come into touch with the central experience of our faith.

Remember! This is a recurring admonition in the writings of Israel and of Christianity. "Remember how for forty years now the Lord has directed all your journeying in the desert" (Dt 8:2). "Be careful not to forget the Lord your God" (Dt 8:11). St. Paul echoes this ancient theme when he exhorts the Christian community at Ephesus: "Do not forget . . . that you had no Christ and were excluded from membership of Israel, aliens without hope and without God. But now in Christ Jesus, you that used to be so far apart from us have been brought very close, by the blood of Christ" (Ep 2:12-13).

Our confidence in God is grounded in his promise never to forget us. Isaiah reassures the exiles that God has not abandoned them. Speaking in God's name he tells them: "Zion was saying, 'Yahweh has abandoned me, the Lord has forgotten me.' Does a woman forget her baby at the breast, or fail to cherish the son of her womb? Yet even if these forget, I will never forget you" (Is 49:14-15).

As his hour drew near, Jesus gathered his friends for the sacred meal. Passover was a feast of remembering the great deeds of Yahweh. In that yearly event the Jewish people relived the most important experience in their history. That night Jesus transformed the meaning of the passover meal into a memorial of his own passage to the Father. It became the supper of the Lord, a celebration of the new and final exodus toward life. Like the ancient feast upon which it was built, the Eucharist is an act of remembering. "Do this in memory of me," Jesus told them. It was not to be an isolated event of history, but a means for Christians throughout history to participate in the pasch of the Lord.

In the biblical context, remembering is the act of making a past experience present in a vital way. When we speak of the tradition of the Church, we are referring to this living memory of faith. Tradition literally means "those things which have been handed on." The tradition is only authentic if it is grounded in the original experience through the faith commitment of later generations. Otherwise it becomes mere custom or empty ceremony. The Christian tradition is a living memory, an ongoing encounter with God. It can only be handed on if it is experienced inwardly. Before it can be passed on to others, it must be personally accepted and internalized by each generation of Christians.

Internalizing the Christian experience is the most pressing task now facing the Church. Today, as in every age, the tradition of the Church is present. It has been handed on to us in the sacred scripture and in the writings of the Church fathers. We possess it in the various creeds and the doctrinal statements which have been formulated in the Church's history. More recently that tradition has been refocused and clarified by scripture scholars and theologians. The Church has enlisted scholars from all over the world to study the development of Christianity from its earliest beginnings. These studies have been a significant factor in updating the Church. The Church has revised its sacramental and liturgical rites so that they will more faithfully reflect and re-present the central mystery of Christianity. The major task of revision is now completed. The Church has a new emphasis that is rooted in the authentic tradition of the Christian gospel.

What is missing? Why has the renewal not developed with the intensity and depth we had originally hoped for?

The missing dimension is inner renewal. It is a question of spirituality. The updated structures will have little effect without the inner renewal of faith. It is true that we have the tradition of Christianity. We have even revised the structures and forms of worship to express that tradition with greater clarity. What is missing is the personal experience of the Christian mystery in our lives. What is missing is the spirituality of the gospel as a motivating energy. We have the tradition as a body of truth, but we have not yet rediscovered our roots. We have the message of the gospel, but we have not come into touch with the "medium" of the gospel—that primordial experience through which it becomes a powerful force in our lives.

An example might clarify this further. Let us suppose that someone decided to renovate the house they had been living in for several years. If

they wanted to remodel the house thoroughly they
might strip it down to the bare structure and begin
to rebuild it. They might replace all the old furni-
ture and carpeting, paint the walls, and hang new
drapes. They might put in all new wiring. Let us
suppose further that they completed the entire
project but never connected it to a source of
electricity. They would have a completely renovated house, with no light, no warmth, no means
of making it a liveable home.

Every example has limitations, but the kernel of
truth remains. The Church is the house we are
talking about. Since the Second Vatican Council
we have been busy with the work of renovation.
The task of refocusing and revising the forms of
worship and the style of authority have been
important and necessary steps in that process of
renewal. But the most important dimension of the
renewal is just beginning. It is the call to inner
renewal and to growth in spirituality. The most
urgent task in the Church today is the challenge to
connect our lives to the "power source," to rediscover our roots and to re-win the spirituality of
the gospel.

Pascal and Personal Renewal

If we can learn from history, perhaps we can
learn from a man named Blaise Pascal. He discovered his roots in the Christian gospel through a
moving experience of personal conversion. This

scientist, philosopher and mystic lived in the 17th Century, in circumstances not unlike our own. He recorded his spiritual pilgrimage in an unpublished manuscript which was later given the title, *Pensees*—Thoughts. In Pascal's life and experience we can see a remarkable similarity with the challenge that faces us today.

Pascal was born and raised in France. He grew up in a civilization which was historically Catholic. But the faith had become more of a cultural habit than a personal commitment. The authentic life of faith was in decline. The French Church had, for the most part, lost touch with its roots in the gospel. There was widespread need for reform and renewal. As spirituality declined, science continued to flourish and expand. Blaise was born into a highly educated family and manifested early signs of genius in the area of science. When he was only twleve years old he had worked out the 32nd theorem of Euclid on his own. By the time he was sixteen he had written a significant treatise on conic sections. At eighteen he began to design and build several computer machines—the forerunners of today's computer. He invented the calculus of probabilities and laid the foundations for advanced algebra. In short, Pascal was one of the greatest scientific geniuses that ever lived. He pushed the human mind to its limits. It was there, at the outer edge of reason, that Blaise became restless for a deeper experience of truth.

On the night of November 23, 1654, Pascal had a religious experience that transformed his life. He describes it in "The Memorial" in these words:

"Fire
'God of Abraham, God of Isaac, God of Jacob,'
not of the philosophers and scientists.
Certitude. Certitude. Feeling. Joy. Peace.
God of Jesus Christ. . . ."[1]

This experience was like an earthquake in Pascal's life. In those two hours he rediscovered the roots of the gospel in his life. He broke through the empty ritual of his age to touch the living memory of faith. He pushed beyond the boundaries of science to encounter God. He moved beyond the God of the philosophers to encounter the living God, the God of Abraham, Isaac, and Jacob, the God of Jesus.

At the time of his conversion Pascal did something extremely significant. He copied the words he had written in his journal onto a small, rectangular piece of cloth. He sewed the cloth on the inside of a cloak which he wore constantly. His intent was clear. He wanted to keep his experience of God alive. He wanted to keep the rediscovery of his roots close to his heart.

There is a significant lesson to be learned from Pascal's life. He tried to put into words his experience of God. He carried his words and his experience close to his heart. This simple gesture creates a symbol of what it means to rediscover our roots. It embodies what Pope John envisioned when he called for a renewal of the Church's life. It is what Danilo's life expresses. Blaise Pascal was a man who literally carried his past into the present with such conviction that he was able to create a new future.

The same call is heard in the Church today. No two people experience God in exactly the same way. Pascal struggled to express his encounter with the God of Abraham, Isaac, and Jacob through his own personality and character. Our response may be different. But there is one thing that we have in common. We are all called to enter into a relationship with God that will change our lives. We have reason to be on fire. We are Christians.

Chapter Four

SET OUT FOR A LAND THAT I WILL SHOW YOU

Journey: The Basis of Spirituality

> Ah, when to the heart of man
>   Was it ever less than a treason
> To go with the drift of things,
>   To yield with a grace to reason,
> And bow and accept the end
>   Of a love or a season?
>
> —Robert Frost

The Experience of Journey

Several years ago I accepted an assignment to pursue graduate studies in Europe. I had always been attracted to the ocean, so I decided to make the journey by boat rather than by plane. Since it was a time of transition for me, I found myself looking forward to the ocean voyage as a time for personal reflection. I also looked forward to the opportunity of experiencing the vastness, the power, and the awesome beauty of the sea.

The passage took ten days and included three stops along the way. Each night before retiring to my cabin I went up to the forward deck. From that vantage point I had a clear view of the sea and the sky. The canopy of stars was brighter than I had ever seen them. The night wind came in gusts and carried the fresh smell of the sea. If it had not been for the deep, steady rumble of the engines several decks below, it would have been difficult for me to believe that we were moving. Only when the occasional lights of another vessel appeared on the horizon and passed us in the distance did I realize that we *were* moving. The dark, star-spangled sky and the immensity of the ocean conveyed the impression that we were a tiny raft drifting on an infinite sea.

But something was moving. Inside me the tide was changing. I felt a persistent restlessness. I was aware of my life moving through time and space. I was lonely.

Was it a fear of the unknown? Was it a feeling of expectancy and anticipation? Was it the intuition that we carry deep within us but cannot put into words, the certainty that life is an unfolding mystery, a story told in footsteps stumbling toward freedom?

In the opening essay of his book, *The Future of Man,* Teilhard de Chardin describes two ways of viewing human life.[1] He pictures the universe as a vast ocean and human beings as passengers on a small raft. From the deck of our vessel we look out toward the horizon and ask ourselves the age-old questions. Are we going anywhere? Is there a destiny for our lives? Are we simply adrift on an infinite sea?

One group of people scans the horizon and answers the questions from their perspective. Nothing is happening, they say. We are not moving in any meaningful direction. We are only drifting. There is no destiny, no sense of newness, no process of development. This group represents the "immobilists" who believe that there is no ultimate goal for human life.

But there is another group on board that also looks out over the sea. They are alive with a restless desire to find meaning. They are not willing to resign themselves to oblivion. They study the horizon with vigilant eyes. They watch the pattern of the waves alongside the raft. They listen attentively to the sound of the night wind. They watch the world with hope. They are not surprised when a shout comes from the lookout: "We are moving!" This group represents those who believe that life is growth. The raft of human existence has a direction. In the sea wind they hear the sounds of newness and the call to destiny. This group experiences life as a mysterious unfolding, a journey toward meaning and fulfillment.

Teilhard uses the image of the raft and the two groups of people as a starting point for an essay on human progress and evolution. He develops a rationale from paleontology and other human sciences that supports the vision of the second group, the "mobilists."

For me, Teilhard's image has a personal meaning. It puts into words an experience that was beneath the surface of my life. I heard it echo in my own feelings as I struggled to answer the eternal questions for myself. The infinity of sea and sky evoked a sense of inner passage. "The river is within us," writes T. S. Eliot, "the sea is all about us." However much we speak of the everlasting hills or the ever-constant sea, our hearts know better. We know that life is in process. From the lookout of our inner selves we see the vision. We speak the words. We are moving! We search the sea that surrounds us, but we touch the river that is within us.

As Christians we have heard the call to be sentries of the Spirit. We stand at the lookout to read the signs of this age. We listen to the wind. We test the pattern of the waves. We study the sea and the sky. We hear the voices of those who say there is no movement, no direction, no goal. But we are unwilling to hand the future over to despair. We wait in the silence of prayer, and, with groping steps, we turn to rediscover our roots. We touch the river that is within us.

What do we touch there? What vision, what conviction about life? What is the starting point of Christian spirituality?

The Journey Theme in Scripture

The scriptures are too rich to be reduced to one theme, too varied to be summarized in a word. The word of God is like a great tapestry in which is woven together the events and encounters, the seeking and the yearning of God and his people. There is one theme, however, which appears in all parts of the tapestry. It is a pattern woven into every design. It underlies all the other themes and

gives them unity. In a word, it is the theme of
journey. It embraces the call to set out, to follow,
to grow, and to move toward a final destiny in
God. The journey theme is the root of Christian
spirituality. It is the unifying theme in the sacred
writings of both Judaism and of Christianity. The
Book of Genesis opens with the Spirit of God
moving across the dark abyss to create order and
peace. The Book of Revelation closes with the
early Christian community waiting in hope for the
final journey, the risen Lord coming in glory to
take his people with him to the Father. Between
Genesis and Revelation there are the many stories
of those who are called to set out on a journey,
those who risk their former life to discover a new
existence.

For the Israelites the Exodus is the decisive
event in their entire history. It is the basis of the
covenant. It establishes the pattern of personal
response to Yahweh. The Exodus event is like the
major theme in a symphony. It recurs throughout
the score. It becomes the creative energy and
vision of sacred history. In the New Testament the
evangelists point to the new exodus of Jesus as the
definitive breakthrough to salvation. The central
event of Christianity is the "passage" of Jesus
through the dark waters of death to new life.
Christian tradition refers to this journey as the
"paschal Mystery." Christian life is the process of
incorporating this mystery into the fabric of our
own life, so that we can say with St. Paul, "I live
now, not I, but Christ lives in me."

If the theme of journey is basic to Christian spirituality, its roots must be deep in the human condition. It must be as deep as the river within us. I want to explore that river of consciousness further, with the hope of clarifying the significance of the journey theme in Christian life.

The Journey Theme in Life

To live is to be in process. Life cannot stand still. It is either developing or dying. When we look for "vital signs," we are attentive to movement, to the alertness of voice or eyes, the squeeze of a hand, the quiet rhythm of breathing, the regular beat of the heart. Even if we can only detect brain waves on an electroencephalogram, we still affirm something of the presence of life.

Death, on the other hand, is the termination of process. The signs of death are rigidity and the cold brittleness that is present at the end of growth. Life is supple with a flexibility that flows from inner movement. We see life's tenderness in the new shoots that appear among patches of snow in the early spring. We see it in the fresh complexion of a young child.

Our experience of journey has its origin in the natural rhythm of biological life. Given certain conditions in the world of nature, the development of life is inevitable.

In human beings growth is dependent upon an additional factor. It is influenced by our *freedom*. In human experience, life moves toward greater inwardness and increased responsibility. Our

growth is more than a process, it is a *passage*. It
is a journey from one level of freedom to another.
Our human growth depends on our attitudes toward life and the choices we make to shape its
meaning. When growth is self-directed, it expresses itself in a series of turning points in which
we either choose to live more fully or turn aside
from growth and, in effect, choose to live less.
These are the peak experiences of our lives. These
are the moments when we are most fully human.

It is freedom, therefore, which gives human life
the form of a journey. Our freedom transforms life
as a process into life as a story. We are the story-
tellers. This is at once the glory and the pain of
being human. We do not measure our lives only by
the seasons of nature. We are more than the sum
of our birthdays. We are more than our medical
profile. We are more than our instruments can
measure or our words can describe. The seasons
of our lives are shaped by the freely chosen
relationships and experiences that make our journey unique. This is true both on the level of our
personal story and in the shared story of the
human community which we call history.

Another reason that our personal development
takes the form of a journey is related to the unique
relationship that we have with *time*. The world of
nature, the plants and animals of the earth,
experience time in relation to the rhythm of biological growth. Nature is *in* time, like an autumn
leaf is caught up in the current of a stream. Time

is both the frame and the background of nature's picture.

As human beings rooted in the earth, we share this experience of being in time. We are limited by its boundaries. We depend upon its constant flow. The process of our biological growth has much of the same inevitability as does the rest of nature. We are born, we grow up, we mature, we reach the prime of our lives, we stretch toward the ripeness of our years, and then we are gone. We may be able to lengthen or shorten the process through technology, but on the biological level the pattern remains fundamentally the same.

Once again it is human freedom that takes us beyond the boundaries of nature. We are not only *in* time, time is in *us*. Time is not only the sea around us; it is the river within us. We direct the flow and pattern of that river by our free choices.

Our use of language reveals the unique manner in which time becomes a part of our personal journey. Human beings are the only creatures who "gain time" or "lose time." We speak of "wasting time," of "making up time," and even of "killing time." Time can "fly" or "drag;" we can have "time on our hands," or be so preoccupied that we "forget what time it is."

Our inner attitudes determine the meaning and quality of time. Our freedom creates the story line in which time becomes *our* journey, *our* passage toward life. It is an ongoing journey because our freedom cannot be fully realized in any one action.

Our decisions are not final. Our lives are un-
finished. We have miles to go before we sleep.

Journey as Death-Resurrection

What is the pattern of growth? What is the
direction of our journey?

We often picture growth as a straight line on an
imaginary graph. We portray it as though it were
a steady process of development. But this picture
holds true only in the abstract. In the real world
the picture is different. Even in the world of
nature, where biological development appears to
be preconditioned by instinct, there is not a steady
flow of progress. Life unfolds in a paradox of
creativity and destruction. Life is always in tension. It achieves growth only through struggle. A
forest fire rages out of control and thousands of
acres are burned. At the same time, the forest fire
creates the possibility of fresh undergrowth and
new timber. A violent hurricane brings havoc to
coastal cities and towns. But it also brings badly
needed rain to the parched farmland further
in nd. The forces of nature move in a world of
paradox.

In the human journey the dimension of struggle
is more evident. Our vision of life is clouded by our
personal contradictions. Our fears and prejudices, our insecurities and needs lock us into
narrow rooms. Our freedom is tentative. Our
choices are not clear. Our growth is shrouded in
ambiguity. Our story is inconclusive.

The human journey is a painful search. It unfolds in the rise and fall of courage. It is the story of breakdowns and breakthroughs, collapses and recoveries. It is a song about failure and healing, a melody of decline and renewal. We leap into the future and we fail. We leave the ruins and begin again. It can be said in simple, direct terms: the human journey is a story of death and resurrection.

In nature we observe this ebb and flow of life in the seasons. We celebrate the rites of spring by picking flowers. We spend our first weekend at the lake. We become "sun worshipers" in July. We come together in thanksgiving at the time of harvest. We gather around a fireplace to watch the dying of another year. We celebrate the stillness of winter and watch the days lengthen toward spring. In the unfolding of the seasons we celebrate life as the rhythm of death and resurrection.

When this rhythm becomes part of the human story we celebrate it as the "rites of passage." These are shared human experiences in which we observe the significant turning points in our life journey. We gather to celebrate the birth of a baby or the death of a friend. We have birthday parties, honor banquets, commencement exercises, and retirement dinners. We hand out cigars and give gold watches. We come together to welcome new neighbors or to say goodbye to old friends who are seeking a new city and a new life.

We mark the stages of the human journey with symbols and signs. We gather at weddings and funerals to share the joy and the sadness of life.

Our journey is lived somewhere between setting out and coming home. In each of the transitional experiences there is a common theme. Human life is a journey of living and dying, of death and resurrection. In each of the rites of passage there is a tension and a release, there is struggle and resolution. There is the paradoxical convergence of light and darkness, growth and decline, life and death. Something dies and is left behind. Something else emerges and breaks through to a new level of realization. Our hearts are restless because they are never totally fulfilled. We are most ourselves when we are leaving the past and setting out toward new horizons. We are most ourselves when we are taking risks for life.

Journey as Inward Transformation

At this point it might be well to summarize the reflections on the pattern of human growth. Human life unfolds in a creative tension between death and resurrection. Its ambiguity is most often expressed in the image of a journey. It is symbolized as a passage from darkness to light, from death to new life.

In the history of human culture this passage is pictured as a physical journey, a change of location. The hero leaves home in search of a treasure or an unknown land. The frightening experiences which he encounters in discovering and conquering the new land constitute the stages of his personal journey. Thus Gilgamesh sets out to discover the secret of immortality at the farthest reaches of the earth. Odysseus struggles through a series of dark adventures in search of his homeland. Orpheus explores the underworld in search of Eurydice. Dante journeys through Inferno, Purgatorio, and Paradiso to find Beatrice.

The scriptural journeys can also be interpreted on this level of outward adventure. Abraham leaves Ur of the Chaldees and sets out for a land that God will show him. Joseph is taken by force into Egypt only to rise to power in that foreign land and provide support for his family in time of crisis. Moses leads the people out of a place of slavery toward a new land flowing with milk and honey. The exiles return to the promised land. Jesus takes the road toward Jerusalem. Saul sets out for Damascus.

Each of these journeys can be understood as a geographical adventure, a search for a new place. In fact, each journey is more than this. From the dawn of culture and religious experience, the journey was understood as more than a change of location. The outward adventure was a symbol of inward search. It is not so much the treasure at the edge of the world that the hero is seeking as it is the truth of his own selfhood. The quest is not the search for new political territory. It is rather the desire to conquer the dark world of human freedom and the recesses of consciousness. It is the journey toward human integration and wholeness, an odyssey of the spirit.

Human awareness grows and deepens. Gradually the outward adventure is interiorized. It becomes the inward journey in search of personal salvation. It is portrayed as the death of the false self and the emergence of the authentic self. The rite of passage becomes the transformation of the inner self through self-emptying and re-integration.

This internalization of the journey theme is especially apparent in the Judeo-Christian tradition. Abraham responded to the call to leave his home and his culture. He is remembered as "the Father of believers" not because he changed geographical locations, but because the outward journey was an image of the inner transformation of his life. Abraham left behind a world of nature worship and polytheism. He risked everything to follow the one, living God, Yahweh. There was a death and a resurrection in his life. At the moment of his setting out, he put aside his old self. A new person began to emerge with every step he took across the desert sands. When Yahweh led his people out of Egypt it was not just to find a more suitable land. It was more than a quest for political freedom. It was a call to leave the way of idolatry and subservience and to become a new people in the desert.

The Tension of Growth

The human heart is the meeting place of contradictions, the ground where life's ambiguities seek to be resolved. We experience our lives as a creative tension. One part of us seeks for new

horizons and experiences. This is the restless
dimension of ourself that stands in wonder and
reaches out to explore life. Another part of us
seeks for rest and the quiet of security. It asks for
clear and final answers. It wants a place to settle
down. If it is forced to move, it wants to build a
permanent dwelling at the next peak or plateau.

The tension between quest and rest is present at
all stages of growth. It is present at the beginning.
Birth is our first experience of death and resurrection. The womb is a secure environment in
which we receive and sustain life in total dependence. Freud described this as "the bliss
before the break." The act of giving birth is a
paradox of pain and joy, agony and ecstasy. It is a
wrenching experience of separation for both
mother and child. The security of the womb, with
its warmth and protection, must be left behind in
order for the child to begin its own process of
growth.

The tension between security and adventure
does not end with birth. It grows with the seasons
and rhythms of the human journey. There is the
familiar picture of the child waiting for the bus on
the first day of school. The fear in her eyes and the
hidden tears of the mother speak of a time of
transition. Both mother and child realize without
saying it that there is no turning back. Life moves
inexorably forward. The child steps on the bus
and begins the long pilgrimage toward adulthood.

At the time of adolescence the tension between
the desire for security and the quest for growth

faces a new crisis. If birth is the experience of physical separation, then adolescence is the leap forward into psychological independence. It is the emotional break from father and mother, the search for personal identity. Adolescence is the dying of the child and the emergence of the adult.

We define our lives by the roads we walk. The choice of a way of life is another turning point in our personal journey. No matter what way of life we choose we are confronted by the mystery of our freedom. We walk through the eye of the paradox. We choose, not once, but each day of our lives. "This is why a man *leaves* his father and mother. . . ." Marriage also is a dying and a rising, a decision to find life in a new relationship and through a new pair of eyes. Marriage does not resolve the dark ambiguities of life. It does not take away the loneliness or quiet the restlessness of our hearts.

The tension between the adventure of freedom and the desire for security haunts us again at middle age. "By the time we are forty," writes Sartre, "we have our face." We have created our vision and our visage out of the complex web of our choices and fears. During the middle years we struggle to accept our limitations, to face our darkness, and acknowledge our failures. We know that there are promises we did not keep and dreams we have forgotten. We feel time passing us by and we are restless to break out of the narrow limitations of our world. We grope toward the light.

The mystery of the human journey reaches its climax at the moment of death. Dying is the most dramatic experience of the tension between security and risk. One part of us clings tenaciously to life. Another part desires to let go and experience death as the final adventure. Our dying will sum up the style of our living. It will be the signature at the bottom of the page, the final choice of our pilgrimage.

The Spirituality of Journey

Spirituality is a vision that arises from the experience of life, a vision that enhances human existence by stretching us beyond our limits. If spirituality were only something superimposed on our life it would not express the full mystery and ambiguity of our pilgrimage. It would not touch the river within us.

As it is, the Word of God has enfleshed itself in the earthy soil of the human condition. The Exodus theme is rooted in the pattern of human growth. It is an event in sacred history which, at the same time, appropriates the human struggle to find life. The spirituality which arises from the journey theme is therefore an integrating vision of human life. It is a spirituality that takes into account all the dimensions of our search. It is a vision that embraces all the dark ambiguities: the pain and the joy, the darkness and the light, the dying and the rising.

The paschal mystery is the redeeming journey of Jesus as he moves through the paradox and ambiguity of human life. In his death and resurrection the contradictions of human life are resolved, not in words, but in the flesh and freedom of the Son of God.

Chapter Five

I HAVE ALWAYS LED A
WANDERER'S LIFE
The Pilgrim God

Tell Us About God

The challenge to grow often comes to us when we are least prepared for it. God speaks in circumstances that we do not plan and through people that we do not choose. "The wind blows where it pleases; you hear its sound, but you cannot tell where it comes from or where it is going. That is how it is with all who are born of the Spirit" (Jn 3:8).

It has taken a long time, but I am beginning to understand the meaning of Jesus' words. I am beginning to look for the Spirit in new places.

I recall being jolted into a renewed search for God by a college student during a weekend retreat. The Second Vatican Council had just come to a close. In its wake there was a widespread feeling of hope, a general mood of optimism. I had recently been assigned to a small Catholic college as chaplain and instructor of philosophy. This was my first opportunity to direct a weekend retreat, and I looked forward to the experience with enthusiasm. I was eager to discuss what I considered to be the crucial issues of the time—the new liturgy, the structures of authority, the role of personal conscience, and the new morality.

To my surprise, the response of the students was less than enthusiastic. They listened to my carefully prepared conferences in respectful silence. But I could see in their eyes that I was not really touching their lives. Halfway through the second day, my voice began to rise and my sentences were edged with determination. Still there was silence. That evening, after I had asked a third time for questions or comments, a young woman looked at me thoughtfully and said, "Father, why don't you just tell us about God?"

It was my turn to be silent. For a few moments I groped for an answer. Then, because words take up time and fill in the dark spaces of our fears, I tried to speak about God. Mostly, I repeated theological ideas that I had read or discussions I had heard in the classroom. I felt as though I were speaking of someone I should know well, but it sounded as if I was reading from an encyclopedia.

The weekend closed with Eucharist. We shared peace and broke the Bread. The students were warm and accepting. We went home.

The young woman's question remained with me. She was a prophetic voice in my life in a way that I did not understand at the time. She raised a question that was to become a challenge to the personal renewal of my faith and spirituality.

Why don't you tell us about God? In the decade after the Second Vatican Council, that question was to become an important issue for the entire Church. The revised forms of the liturgy and the problems of authority are still significant issues in the life of the Church. They must continue to be discussed, but they are not *the* issue. The role of personal conscience and the new morality are important questions today. They must continue to be asked, but they are not *the* question.

Why don't you tell us about God? *That* is the real issue. The answer to that question is crucial to the work of renewal. It is an answer that can arise only from the experience of God in prayer, in faith, and in community. It is an answer that can arise only through a rediscovery of the God of journey, the pilgrim God of biblical experience.

Why don't you tell us about God? After several years of being haunted by that question, I have finally begun to understand it as a question. I understand it because it is now *my* question. These days I wonder less about the structures of the Church and more about God. I seek the answer to that question not so much in the realm of theological debate as in the search for a renewed spirituality. It has become a question of faith.

I suspect that my experience reflects that of many others in the Church today. We began the renewal thinking in terms of updating the Church as though it were a presence outside ourselves that needed to be renovated and given a new face. We thought that the renewal was a process of reorganization and revision. We are only now learning that it is a call to personal conversion. The Spirit blows where he pleases. The wind of God has found its way into our locked rooms where we waited in fear or in complacency. He has

touched our hearts with fire. He has raised the
eternal questions. He has driven us back to faith.
It is our own hearts that need to be reshaped and
reformed. We are seeking again for the living God.

What Can We Say About God?

Why don't you tell us about God? What answer
do we give to this question? What can we say
about God in our time?

We can say that we grew up believing in God
because faith was given to us as infants. We can
say that we became adults on the day that God
ceased to be a given and became a question. We
can say that we have experienced doubts about
his presence and his role in our lives. We can say
that a century of war and human suffering has
cast a shadow over his existence. We can say that
we have studied Nietzsche in college and read
about the "death of God." We can say that we
have discussed Freud's theory of God as a pro-
jection of the father figure. We can say that we
have reassessed our faith in the light of the
Marxist critique of religion. We can say that we
have attended lectures in which religion was
portrayed as a source of pathological guilt.

Today we can even say positive things about the
place of God in our society. We can say that the
death of God movement has come and gone, and
that faith is still flourishing. We can say that Jung
has replaced Freud, and that psychology now
recognizes a creative role for religious experience
in human life. We can say that Marxists and

Christians have entered into serious dialogue. We can say that there are large numbers of people who practice transcendental meditation and who seek for the infinite.

We could say all this and more, but we still would not have faced the real question. Jesus once asked his disciples what the crowds were saying about him. In response Peter recounted the current popular opinions about Jesus. But Jesus became more direct. His question was a personal one. "But you," he said, "who do you say I am" (Mt 16:15)? The quest for spirituality becomes direct and personal in this same way. The question involves our own commitment, not just that of our society. "Who am I to you?," Jesus is asking us. "What difference do I make in your life?" The question is not what we consider to be the latest belief about God. The question is what can we say about God from our lives and from the living tradition of our religious heritage? How does he reveal himself to us? Who is the God of Abraham, Isaac and Jacob? Who is the God of Jesus? Who is the God of the Christian community? Who is the God of my life?

To answer these questions we must go beyond theological explanations and turn to the experience of God in prayer and faith. We must explore the unfolding mystery of God in the consciousness of his people. We must rediscover our roots in the biblical tradition. We must encounter the God of the desert and of the Exodus.

In sacred history, God reveals himself as a

transcendent presence who calls us by name. He reveals himself as a personal presence who invites us into covenant with him and with one another. Most of all, he reveals himself as *Abba*, the Father of Jesus, the loving presence in the midst of life, who calls us to journey with him toward everlasting communion.

The renewal of the Church depends on the personal rediscovery of Christian spirituality. The search for spirituality, in turn, is rooted in the experience of God as the call to growth.

Rediscovering the God of Our Fathers

Moses can be considered as a model in our search to rediscover God in our lives. Moses was born a Hebrew, but he grew up as an Egyptian. At that time Egypt was considered to be the most advanced civilization in the world. In the Acts of the Apostles (7:22), St. Luke tells us that Moses was educated in the culture and wisdom of the Egyptian people. He knew their laws and appreciated their literature. He studied their science and became skilled in their methods of political administration.

The Book of Exodus seems to assume that Moses had some role in government, perhaps in regard to his fellow Hebrews who were slaves. Moses' relationship to the Hebrew tradition was by blood only. He had very little knowledge of their religious heritage or experience. Like many of the Hebrew slaves, Moses had lost touch with the God of his Fathers, the God of Abraham, Isaac and Jacob.

Moses first became concerned about his people when he left the court of the Pharaoh and toured the provinces. There he saw firsthand the oppressed condition of the Hebrew slaves. In a burst of anger, he killed an Egyptian who was beating a Hebrew slave. The next day when he reprimanded two Hebrews for quarrelling, they rejected his intervention and indicated that his action of the previous day was widely known. Moses realized that his life was in danger. He knew that he was a man without true identity and without roots. He fled into the desert.

Moses' journey into the wilderness proved to be more than a flight toward safety. It was the turning point of his life. In the desert, Moses rediscovered the God of his fathers.

Moses married one of Jethro's daughters and became a nomad like his ancestors. While following the flocks of the Midianites to the far side of the wilderness, he approached what was probably one of the ancient desert sanctuaries of the Hebrews near Mt. Horeb. There, at the foot of the mountain of God, Moses had what can only be described as a mystical experience. In the loneliness of exile he heard the sound of his name. He saw before him a blazing desert bush that appeared to burn without being consumed. He heard his name called again.

"Here I am," Moses responded.

"Come no nearer," the Voice said, "take off your shoes for the place in which you stand is holy ground. I am the God of your father, the God of Abraham, the God of Isaac and the God of Jacob" (Ex 3:4-6).

In the wilderness Moses rediscovered the God of his fathers. He had to leave behind the advanced civilization of Egypt and become a nomad before he could touch his roots. He had to become a pilgrim in order to discover his identity. In the desert Moses was transformed from a concerned government official into a prophetic leader. The key to his conversion was his personal encounter with God. In that meeting Moses saw the condition of his people with new clarity. He realized that the slavery of his people was more than political oppression. The real tragedy lay in the fact that they had been cut off from their religious roots. They had lost the experience of God in their lives. They would not be liberated until they, too, had returned to the desert.

The call and the presence of Yahweh entered the life of Moses. The flame in the bush became the fire in his eyes and in his heart. He would not rest until he had led his people out of Egypt into the desert to the foot of this same mountain. He would not rest until his people had rediscovered the God of their fathers.

Like Moses, we, too, are in search of our roots. We have grown up in a culture whose values are often alien to those of the gospel. We have become strangers in our own land. We are exiles of the spirit. We know that all is not well with ourselves and with our brothers and sisters. The quest for spirituality today leads us back to the desert and to the burning bush. It summons us to re-win our roots in the biblical tradition. It challenges us to encounter the God of Jesus, the new Moses, who leads us in the new exodus to communion with the Father.

The Pilgrim God

What can we say about God? We can say that he is a God who calls us to personal pilgrimage. He is the Lord who summons Abraham to leave behind the nature gods of his culture and to follow a promise into the future. He is the God of Moses who calls us to personal liberation and to a covenant bond of love.

God not only calls his people to become nomads of the spirit. He is himself a God of Journey. He is a pilgrim God who breaks into the endless cycles of nature and transforms them into sacred history. He is a God of process and of growth who calls his people to share a journey toward life.

Exodus pictures Yahweh as a fellow pilgrim. "God led the people by the roundabout way of the wilderness to the sea of Reeds" (Ex 13:17). It emphasizes that Yahweh went *before* his people: "Yahweh went before them, by day in the form of a pillar of cloud to show them the way, and by night in the form of a pillar of fire to give them light: thus they could continue their march by day and by night" (Ex 13:21).

Unlike the nature gods of the surrounding cultures, the God of the Israelites is not limited to a particular place or to a season of the year. He is not contained by any sanctuary or temple. He moves with his people. His dwelling place is a tent.

The Israelites described their God in terms of his companionship with them. One of the most meaningful of these descriptions is the image of the shepherd. This image arose from their nomadic way of life. This people who were skilled in the gentle and courageous art of shepherding their flocks, see themselves, in turn, as the flock of Yahweh, their Shepherd. Shepherding is a symbol of mobility. The God of Israel reveals himself to us as a desert God, a pilgrim Lord who moves through the wilderness with his people.

The God of Tents and Exiles

We have already discussed the natural tension between the desire for security and the spirit of adventure. This same tension is found in the religious life of the people of Israel after they reach the promised land. As they became more settled in Palestine, the Israelites began to pattern many aspects of their culture after the nations that surrounded them. Their leader became a king. Their faith became more ritualized and less centered in the desert covenant. The priesthood rose to power and the laws regarding worship and ritual purification multiplied. The people lost much of their nomadic spirit. They settled down to a religious life that frequently emphasized external observance at the expense of the inner attitude of faith.

But Yahweh continued to call his people to growth. As the Israelites reached out to embrace more comfortable forms of religion, God challenged them to inward renewal through the prophets.

A significant instance of this takes place during the reign of David. One day David sat in his palace and looked around at the luxurious surroundings which he enjoyed. The Israelite people had come a long way since their nomadic wanderings in the desert. They were now a political power to be reckoned with, a nation among nations, with a strong army, a centralized government, and a king.

But the king was restless. He called in the prophet, Nathan, and said, "Look, I am living in a house of cedar while the ark of God dwells in a tent." In his mind, David had begun to plan a magnificent temple for the Lord.

That night God spoke to Nathan: "Go and tell my servant David, 'Thus Yahweh speaks: Are you the man to build me a house to dwell in? I have never stayed in a house from the day I brought the Israelites out of Egypt until today, but have always led a wanderer's life in a tent. In all my journeying with the whole people of Israel, did I say to any one of the judges of Israel, whom I had appointed as shepherds of Israel my people: Why have you not built me a house of cedar'" (II S 7:5-7)?

Then Yahweh revealed his plan to build a house

for David (II S 7:12). It will not be a house of cedar
or a temple of gold. It will be a people. The
dwelling place of Yahweh will be a community of
faith, a people of promise, who, like their God, will
live in pilgrimage.

There are some political overtones in Nathan's
prophecy. He is speaking for the religious tradition that still looked to the desert as the model for
Israel's life of worship. But this opposition to the
temple soon faded and its construction was begun
and completed under Solomon. The value of
Nathan's prophecy lies not in its political implications but in what it reveals about God and his
relationship with his people.

Pilgrimage is not an accidental characteristic of
Yahweh. He is by nature a God of journey. The
divine presence cannot be identified with the
structure of the temple. It is not limited to the
priestly class or contained in the ritual laws of
worship and purification. God is eternal growth
and eternal discovery. He calls the human spirit to
break out of the narrow vision of security and to
follow him into the mystery of the future. The
exodus is more than an event. It is a way of living
and believing, a way of walking with God.

Whenever the people choose the settled life of
comfortable ritual, God calls them back to pilgrimage. Whenever they limit the covenant to
external forms of worship or to a token observance of the law, he raises up prophets to call
them back to the desert road.

This is also the message of Ezechiel, the prophet of the exile. The fall of Jerusalem in 597 B.C. came as a death blow to those who identified God's presence with the temple and its institutions. The sanctuary of Yahweh was desecrated, the priesthood was dispersed, and the religious heritage of the people was left in ruins.

Ezechiel, the son of Buzi, was one of the exiles taken into Babylonia in the first deportation. With his fellow refugees he settled along the banks of the river Chebar. Ezechiel probably belonged to the aristocracy of Jerusalem. He may even have been a member of the priestly class.

This background information makes Ezechiel's prophecy all the more remarkable. He recounts his call to be a prophet in an extraordinary vision which he had while in exile. Ezechiel describes how he saw Yahweh seated upon his throne in the Holy of Holies. His vision is charged with strange sights and sounds: the storm with its flashes of lightning, the four creatures, the faces and the wings, the gleaming wheels and the sound of rushing water. If we go beyond the imaginative language, there are two important truths that emerge from Ezechiel's vision. First, God's presence is experienced as *mobile*. He rides in a heavenly chariot. Secondly, Yahweh is pictured as coming to be with the exiles along the river Chebar.

Ezechiel shares a vision of consolation and hope with his brothers and sisters in exile. He assures them that Yahweh is still a pilgrim God. He is not limited to the temple or its priesthood. He is not confined to the ritual sacrifices and laws as practiced in Jerusalem. Yahweh is a transcendent nomad. He comes to be with his people. As once he led them toward freedom, so now he comes to share their exile and to lead them home in a new exodus.

The prophecies of Nathan and Ezechiel reveal the persistent struggle in Israel between the desire for human security and the call to grow in the Spirit. We see this tension in the confrontation between priesthood and prophecy. We see it in the struggle between institution and personal charism. We find it in the tension between outward observance and inward faith.

He Pitched His Tent With Us

This is the same tension which Jesus confronted in his public ministry and which eventually led to his death. Jesus challenged the Scribes and the Pharisees to re-win the spirituality of the desert. He confronted the religious leaders with their failure to hear the cry of the prophets for renewal. He condemned them for turning the wilderness covenant into a maze of laws and meaningless ritual. He declared that he had not come to destroy the religious vision of his people but to fulfill it and to bring it to perfection in his own life.

Jesus' dedication to his vision of renewal led, at times, to drastic action. In a burst of anger he entered his Father's house and drove out the buyers and the sellers. "The Jews intervened and said, 'What sign can you show us to justify what you have done?' Jesus answered, 'Destroy this sanctuary, and in three days I will raise it up.' The Jews replied, 'It has taken forty-six years to build this sanctuary: are you going to raise it up in three days' " (Jn 2:18-20)?

The encounter between Jesus and the Jewish leaders ends with this comment: "But he [Jesus] was speaking of the sanctuary of his body" (Jn 2:21). An age old dream is about to come true. Jesus promises to fulfill the prophecy which Nathan spoke to David many centuries before. Jesus will build a house for humanity. He is the dwelling place of the Father, and his followers will become the temple of the Spirit (Co 6:19; Rm 8:11). In Jesus, God has come to live with his people.

"The Word became flesh and dwelt among us" (Jn 1:14). If we were to translate these words from the proloque of John literally, they would read: "And the Word became flesh and *pitched his tent with us.*" Jesus is the pilgrim presence of God in the midst of his people. His risen body, the Church, is the temple of his Spirit. We are the new Israel moving with God toward the final destiny of history.

The Search for God Today

As we seek for a renewed vision of spirituality in the Church today, we find ourselves returning

to the biblical roots of our faith, to the God of our
fathers, and to the God of Jesus, our brother. We
have heard the call to rediscover the pilgrim God.

We also wrestle with the same temptation that
haunted the Israelite people in their long history.
We are hesitant pilgrims. In our fear we often
enshrine the structures of security rather than
follow God into the wilderness. We want to open
ourselves to a renewed experience of God, but at
the same time we cling to attitudes which prevent
us from being pilgrim people.

Our response to the Second Vatican Council is a
good example of this ambiguity. The council was a
breakthrough of the Spirit. The statements of the
council and the subsequent enactments reflect a
more biblical understanding of God and of the
Church. But Vatican II was only a beginning, not a
conclusion. It will be remembered not for the new
structures it gave us, so much as for the vision it
provides for the future. We have seen the vision.
There is not yet a clear response to its implications.

The Church stands at the edge of the desert.
Some of its members look back wistfully to the
security of the past. Others are impatient to set
out into the wilderness. We live in the season of
uncertainty. The Church has yet to decide
whether it will be a beacon or a boundary.

In the meantime we seek for the pilgrim Lord in
our midst. The technological revolution and the
historical events of our age have created a crisis
of faith. They have also had a purifying effect in

our lives. The increased responsibility which we
feel for shaping history has brought us much
closer to the biblical vision of God. God revealed
himself to the Israelites as a God of history rather
than as a God of nature. He invited them to share
in the task of creating the future and of becoming
"a light to the nations." We are conscious that the
burden of the future is on our shoulders. This
emergence of a sense of history is one of the signs
of our age. It can lead us to a more biblical understanding of God. God reveals himself to us not as a
God *above* us but as a God *before* us. The theologians of hope describe God as "the future of
man." God is at once the destiny of our lives and
our companion along the way.

What can we say about God?

We can say that he is the God of Abraham—the
God of journey. He is the summons in life to leave
the idols behind and to set out into the unknown.
This God calls us to risk security for the sake of
discovery. He promises to show us the landscape
of the Spirit and walk with us through the wilderness of our hearts. The God of Abraham makes
promises and keeps them. He is a faithful God.
When we follow his call we must walk by the dark
light of faith. We must entrust our lives to him in a
covenant of love. We must be willing to pass
through the land of "terrifying darkness" (Gn
15:12) and doubt. We encounter the God of
Abraham when we follow the wilderness road that
leads to life.

What can we say about God?

We can say that he is the God of Isaac—the God
of laughter. He is the God who moves beyond our
calculations and plans to surprise us with the
impossible. He is the God of paradox. He is the
God who gives life in times and places that we
have pronounced as dead. The God of Isaac is the
call to wonder. He gives us eyes that are wide
enough to look at our contradictions without
squinting. He is the unconquerable energy of hope
that smiles through our tears. The God of Isaac
gives us the freedom to laugh at ourselves. Someday he will have the last laugh. He will see it in our
eyes and hear it on our lips.

What can we say about God?

We can say that he is the God of Jacob—the God
of struggle. He is the God who wrestles with us in
the night of our growth. He is the God of our
broken dreams, the Lord of the absurd. We
thought it was the dark shadows of our despair
that we fought. It turned out to be God. We clung
to him then and demanded to know his name. But
it was he who named us and reshaped our lives.
We are Jacob in the process of becoming Israel.
God will not let us give in to the night. He wrestles
us toward the edge of dawn. In the morning light,
as we limp away, we are not sure who has won.
We only remember that at some moment the
struggle went beyond desperation to playfulness,
beyond agony to ecstasy. It was a long night. We
feel a new strength inside.

What can we say about God?

We can speak of him in the language of philosophy or measure him in the instruments of science. We can reflect on his presence in psycology or explore the world of art and poetry to find his face. We can turn to the themes of theology and to the accounts of the mystics. In the end we lapse into silence. In the stillness of prayer we listen to him in the language of his own Word. We describe God best when we speak of him as the God of Abraham, Isaac and Jacob. And when we speak this language, the language of scripture, we discover that we are describing our own encounter with mystery. We find words for our call to journey and to hope. We find phrases for the night of our doubt.

What can we say about God?

We can say that he is the God of Journey, Laughter, and Struggle.

Chapter Six

AS THOSE WHO ARE IN FLIGHT
The Pilgrim People

"This is what Yahweh asks of you:
only this, to act justly,
to love tenderly
and to walk humbly with your God"

(Mi 6:8)

Watching Things Grow

It is March—the month of lambs and wolves and changing skies. In the yard there are patches of snow and green grass. The snow maintains it is winter, but the grass is pushing up spring.

My grandmother sits in her chair by the window and looks at the changing face of the world. She is silver-haired and silent. Her hearing has faded in the last several years, but her sensitivity to life has not changed. She is a sentry of the Spirit watching for new life.

I have watched her like this many times. I have seen her gazing quietly out the window for hours. This time I move closer to her and ask, "Grandma, what do you think about as you look out the window?"

She turns toward me, smiles and says, "I think about your grandad and all the seasons that have come and gone. I remember the past and I wait for the Lord. And while I wait, I like to watch things grow."

Grandma has seen a lot of things grow in her life. Her family came from St. John's Province in Quebec. She and my grandfather homesteaded in North Dakota. She has worked the land, raised a family, and watched many winters turn to spring. Now arthritis makes walking difficult and painful for her. But it hasn't affected the restlessness of her heart. Grandma is still a pilgrim.

Remembering the past . . . Waiting for the Lord . . . Watching things grow. It is a diary of the human condition. I look at Grandma and I realize, with new insight, that we are all immigrants and homesteaders.

We are immigrants not only because our ancestors came from other lands, but because we are always on the way toward life. We are immigrants because we have no lasting home, and because, like my grandmother, our hearts keep on moving long after our feet stop walking.

We are homesteaders because we take risks for life. We cross oceans and prairies to explore new territory. We look at the moon and want to go there. We set out to discover new land to clear and new earth to plow. We are homesteaders because someday we will sit beside a window and watch spring come, while our hearts move on to find God.

God's Immigrants

God chose a people who like to watch things grow. He entered the mainstream of human life through the experience of an immigrant people, a people who crossed seas and deserts to find the future; a people who remembered their past and celebrated it as a promise of things to come; a people who, through long centuries, learned to wait for God.

I understood something essential about belonging to this people when I watched my Grandmother at the window. I realized that the people of God are created in the image of their maker. Like the God who leads us, we, too, are pilgrims.

Reflecting on the mystery of God's ways, Chesterton once commented: "How odd of God to choose the Jews." His statement catches some of the playfulness of divine providence. There is a smile behind sacred history.

When we view the Judao-Christian experience from the panorama of world history, it appears strange indeed that God chose a band of wandering tribes to be his special people. How odd of God to choose a group of nomads who were not politically strong enough to build an empire. How strange that he selected a people who were considered outcasts by the surrounding nations. The Hebrew people wandered along the edges of the wilderness and then settled at the crossroads of civilization. Because of their vulnerability, they were conquered by every major mideastern civilization that rose to power.

How odd of God to choose the Jews. By human standards, yes. In the plan of God, no. History might find it mysterious, but faith sees the hand of love.

Faith does not demand that we smooth over the paradox of sacred history. We need not deny the political power. Their journey of faith could not be contained by borders.

When the Israelites boasted, it was on God's behalf. They kept the admonition of Deuteronomy close to their hearts: "If Yahweh set his heart on you and chose you, it was not because you outnumbered other peoples: you were the least of all peoples. It was for love of you and to keep the oath he swore to your fathers that Yahweh brought you out with his mighty hand and redeemed you from the house of slavery, from the power of Pharaoh king of Egypt. Know then that Yahweh your God is God indeed, the faithful God who is true to his covenant and his graciousness for a thousand generations towards those who love him and keep his commandments" (Dt 7:7-9).

Faith sees farther than the history of empires. It is the vision and heritage of the Hebrews that we have inherited, not that of their conquerors. We may admire the military genius of Alexander. We may respect the culture of the Egyptians. But we worship the God of Abraham and David, the God of Moses and Jesus. We are descendants of Abraham. We find life in the same journey of faith. God loves us because we are immigrants.

The church today recognizes and celebrates its continuity with this nomadic people. The second Vatican Council describes the Church as "the new People of God." It characterizes the Church in the same terms with which the Israelites understood their identity and mission: "This messianic people, although it does not include all men, and may more than once look like a small flock, is nonetheless a lasting and sure seed of unity, hope and salvation for the whole human race" (*Lumen Gentium*, #9).

Our continuity with the Hebrew people is the soil out of which a contemporary spirituality of journey can grow. We have reflected on the pilgrim God. Let us now explore the faith journey of his people.

The Habiru: God's Chosen Ones

Who are the Hebrew people?

The word in Aramaic is *habiru*. This term does not refer to "the Hebrews" as we are familiar with them in the pages of scripture. Until the time of the captivity the term *habiru* was not used as a common name for a particular ethnic or racial group. It was a colorful, somewhat pejorative name to describe any nomadic people who wandered on the edges of the desert in search of grazing land and water for their flocks. Biblical experts give various translations for the term. Some maintain that it means "the dusty ones," probably referring to the appearance of the caravans, the donkey drivers, or the slave laborers. Sometimes it is even used in reference to fugitives and outlaws.

Habiru can also be translated as "one who has crossed over." In Genesis it is consistently applied to those who sojourn as strangers in a land which is not their native country. Thus Abraham is referred to as a *habiru* while he is living near Mamre (Gn 14:13). Joseph is given the same title when is is in Egypt (Gn 39:14; 41:12).

Whatever the origin and meaning of the word, it came to be applied to any group of people who were nomads and strangers. It characterizes those who are of a lower class and who wander on the fringe of civilization. The *habiru* were the outcasts of the ancient mideastern world. Later the term came to be identified with the Israelites.

What's in a name? In the biblical world a name was more than a label. It expressed the identity and meaning of its bearer, and spoke of promises to be kept and roads to be walked. Sometimes a name is given in derision. Friends give names of endearment. Strangers may name their enemies out of fear. Later, that same name may be adopted in a spirit of defiance and carried with a sense of pride. This probably is the case with the Hebrews. God chose the scattered tribes that trace their origin in some way back to Abraham. Other nations had pushed them aside or conquered them, ignored them or laughed at them for centuries. But in the Exodus experience the *habiru* achieved a new identity and a new pride. In the wilderness God sent this message to the people through Moses: "Say this to the House of Jacob, declare this to the sons of Israel, 'you yourselves have seen what I did with the Egyptians, how I carried you on eagle's wings and brought you to myself. From this you know that now, if you obey my voice and hold fast to my covenant, you of all nations shall be my very own for all the earth is mine. I will count you a kingdom of priests, a consecrated nation'" (Ex 19:3-6).

The experience of being chosen by God transformed the vision and identity of the *habiru*. They continued to be wanderers but now it was with a new sense of destiny. They committed themselves to Yahweh with fierce pride and deep trust. They were more than desert nomads now. They were God's pilgrim people.

The *habiru* were the original "counter-culturalists." They lived on the outskirts of civilization and refused to settle down to the comfortable religion of the other cultures. It was only after the Hebrews settled in the promised land that many of them turned aside from their nomadic roots and sought to model their way of life after the surrounding nations, especially the Canaanite culture.

The Habiru and the Canaanites:
The Tension of Faith

The Canaanites had a static, comfortable religion based on the rhythm of the seasons and the physical needs of human life. Their religion was not a vision of faith but simply a ritualization of nature's cycles. The Canaanite religion found security in being in harmony with the earth. It was a "good time" religion that observed the moments of growth and harvest and worshipped the creative powers of life. There was little or no room for suffering or pain or journey in this religion. It was not a way for pilgrims.

The Hebrews were strongly influenced by the Canaanite world. It affected their language and gave them the basic tools of science. It provided models for agriculture and for political organization. But it also threatened their covenant with Yahweh.

The Canaanite religion was an invitation to settle for security. It tempted the human spirit to adjust itself to the physical and emotional needs of nature. It was the choice to stop walking and the decision to be identified with the cycles of the earth. God called Abraham to go beyond the cycles of nature to share in the adventure of sacred history. To follow the Canaanite religion would involve a choice to reverse the journey of Abraham. It would mean turning aside from the wilderness road. It would be a betrayal of the call to pilgrimage.

The persistent demand of the prophets was a call to reject the Canaanite nature gods and to turn back to the pilgrim God. The prophets challenged the Hebrews to return to the experience of the Exodus.

In order to make their message effective, the prophets relived the exodus experience in their own lives. On the edge of despair, Elijah made the desert journey back to Mt. Horeb in search of the God of his fathers. Jeremiah encountered his desert in the persecution he suffered at the hands of the political and religious establishment of his time. He also wrestled with the darkness of his depression and loneliness. Ezechiel discovered the pilgrim God coming to be with his exiles and leading them back to life. John the Baptist, the last and greatest prophet, also returned to the desert to challenge the people to repentance. In his stark figure there is the echo of an earlier cry from Isaiah: "A voice cries in the wilderness: Prepare a way for the Lord, make his paths straight. Every valley will be filled in, every mountain and hill be laid low, winding ways will be straightened and rough roads made smooth. And all mankind shall see the salvation of God" (Lk 3:5; of Is 40:3-5).

The Passover: Call to Freedom

The central religious experience for the Hebrews was the Exodus. In that event their aimless wandering became a pilgrimage toward life. In the desert covenant they achieved their identity as a people. Yahweh became their God and they became his people.

As the Canaanites celebrated the rites of passage in nature, so the Hebrews celebrated their passage from slavery to freedom. The ceremony which ritualized this turning point in their history was the feast of the Passover. In this celebration the Exodus was recalled as a present experience in the life of the people. The Passover also celebrated their hope in the future. The journey goes on. The final destiny is in the future.

Our English word, "passover," is derived from the Greek, *pascha* (hence our term, pasch or paschal). It is in turn taken from the Hebrew word, *pesah*. Like many other biblical terms, the origin of *pesah* is disputed. It is usually associated with the verb, *pasah*—to pass over or to spare. But it can also mean to limp or to leap.

Originally, *pesah* referred to God's saving act of "passing over" the houses of the Israelites on the night of the last plague. The angel of the Lord struck down the first born of the Egyptians, but he spared the lives of the Hebrews.

Eventually the passover was applied to the entire experience of the Exodus. It included not only Yahweh's passage in the night, but also the passage of the Hebrews from slavery to freedom. Passover became an all-inclusive term to describe the journey of God's people through the dark waters toward a new land. It is the passage from darkness to light, from death to new life. Passover is the call to liberation and personal transformation in the wilderness.

It is significant that the Hebrew word for passover carries with it a certain ambiguity. The most fundamental experiences of our lives touch the depth of our humanity. There we discover that the categories of science or rationality are no longer adequate. We enter the world of symbol and mystery. We are confronted with paradox. *Pasah* carries with it the ambiguity of strength and weakness. It implies that the journey toward freedom is painful but full of promise. We make the passage in fear and brokenness. We limp toward life. But our limping becomes a leap toward freedom. On the road to life we dance for joy. *Pasah* is the Hebrew way of speaking about death and resurrection.

The Passover: Feast of Journey

The celebration of our faith in worship does not drop down ready made from heaven. Liturgy emerges from human experience which has been transformed by the saving action of God. With the eyes of faith we view the human pilgrimage from a new perspective. We see it as a journey with God toward life. We should be neither surprised nor scandalized that the Judao-Christian tradition is a transformation of the human search for meaning. Grace builds on nature. The Word becomes flesh. Our worship ritualizes the peak experiences of the human journey. It enhances, enriches and expands our understanding of our lives by creating symbols that go beyond our words.

The feast of the Passover is a good example of this transformation of human experience into faith symbols. The passover celebration as a human ritual is found much earlier than God's saving intervention in Egypt. The Exodus event gave the Hebrews a new perspective through which they transformed the meaning of their ancient nomadic rituals into experiences of worship.

The passover meal as it is outlined in the Book of Exodus is actually a joining together of two ancient celebrations. One is the nomadic celebration of the lamb; the other is the agricultural feast of the unleavened bread.

The nomadic feast has its origins in the tribal setting of the ancient mideast. Before the *habiru* had come to believe in the God of Abraham or Moses they celebrated a springtime feast centered around the ritual sacrifice and eating of a lamb from their flocks. The evidence that is available suggests that it was a family festival celebrated at the full moon of the vernal equinox. A young animal born that year was offered to the divinity to insure prosperity and growth in the flocks and to obtain divine protection in finding new pasture-land.

To appreciate the significance of this ritual we must use our imagination and enter into the life experience of the nomadic peoples. The tribes waited during the long dry season for the new rain and the promise of growth. As the food dwindled and the pastureland disappeared, many died from lack of nourishment. The coming of spring was the only hope of survival. For the nomadic tribes it was not just another time of the year, it was the moment of life or death.

The first full moon of springtime was reverenced as the sacred time. It was the moment of new beginnings, the hour of setting out. With all their belongings packed, the tribal families gathered in their tents to celebrate a new beginning. After ritually killing one of the young lambs, they smeared some of the blood on their tent posts. The purpose of this was to drive away any evil spirits and to insure protection for the flocks. The *habiru* then roasted the lamb and shared a meal of celebration. When the meal was finished, they set out in the moonlight in search of new pastures.

Year after year, the *habiru* celebrated this ritual. Generation after generation gathered at their tents, shared the meal, and then walked toward life. The feast of the lamb was an essential part of their way of life. It celebrated the purpose of their wanderings and gave meaning to the restlessness of their hearts.

The feast of the Unleavened Bread was originally distinct from the Passover. It was an agrarian feast celebrating the beginning of the spring harvest. It lasted seven days during which time bread was made from the new grain. The leaven from the previous year was removed as a rite of purity and as a symbol of the annual renewal of the earth. The feast celebrated the death and resurrection of nature and invited the people to participate in life's continued productivity. Since the new flour could not be mixed with the old, the bread was initially unleavened.

The feast of the Unleavened Bread reflected a more agricultural setting, but its meaning was somewhat similar to that of the Passover. It became associated with the Passover feast because it also was a springtime celebration. Eventually the two became one feast.

When the Hebrews were led out of Egypt by Yahweh, they interpreted this saving event in the light of their nomadic background. God's intervention transformed the meaning of their wandering and the significance of their religious ritual.

That spring night, as they set out toward the sea and the desert, they realized that something awesome was taking place in their lives. They were not just going in search of new pastures as their fathers had done. They were not just beginning a new season of grazing for their flocks. They were going in search of freedom. They were setting out to encounter the God of their fathers in the desert. Nothing would ever again be the same. Their journey would transcend the cycles of nature and become part of sacred history.

Thus, the Passover meal was transformed from a nomadic feast of springtime into a celebration of God's saving deed in history. After the Hebrews settled in the promised land, the feast of Unleavened Bread was eventually incorporated into the rite of the Passover. Many of the elements and customs of the original celebrations were retained in the new rite: the killing and roasting of the lamb, the blood on the doorposts, the unleavened bread, the bitter herbs, and the meal shared in a family setting.

But the meaning of the feast was radically changed. All the former elements were related in some way to the historical event of the Exodus. The blood of the lamb became a symbol of salvation from death; the bitter herbs reminded the people of their past slavery; and the unleavened bread recalled the haste with which they left Egypt. The entire celebration was centered around the presence of Yahweh. It was a celebration of his power and care for his people. This is reflected in the directions given for the meal in the book of Exodus: "This is the way you must eat the meal: you shall have your belts fastened, your sandals on your feet and your staff in your hand. You must eat as those who are in flight. It is the Lord's passover" (Ex 12:11, my translation).

The Anawim: Pilgrims in Exile

The spirituality of the Exodus continued to be the sustaining vision of Israel. During the time of the kings, the priesthood became corrupt and the covenant was reduced to mere lip service. The prophets confronted the leaders and the people with their failure to follow Yahweh, and challenged them to return to the spirituality of the desert.

Finally, after years of political corruption and infidelity to God, the divided kingdoms fell to foreign powers. Large numbers of people were taken into exile. The Israelites returned to the original condition of the *habiru*. They became outcasts. In a few short years their vision of the future seemed to collapse. The suffering of the people was widespread. Many of the Hebrews despaired or turned to other religions.

However painful and humiliating the exile was, it also had a purifying effect. During these dark years a new vision of spirituality emerged. The prophets had frequently spoken of a "remnant" who would remain faithful to Yahweh and to the desert covenant. During the exile this faithful remnant came into being. A small, politically insignificant group of people continued to trust in the Lord in the face of every adversity. They became known as the *anawim*, "the little ones," the humble, followers of the living God. The *anawim* refused to compromise their faith or their way of life in the midst of an alien culture. They were the new *habiru*, the new outcasts of God. We hear their plaintive cry in Psalm 137:

> Beside the streams of Babylon
> we sat and wept
> at the memory of Zion,
> leaving our harps
> hanging on the poplars there.
>
> For we had been asked
> to sing to our captors,
> to entertain those who had carried us off:
> 'Sing' they said
> 'some hymns of Zion.'
>
> How could we sing
> one of Yahweh's hymns
> in a pagan country?
> Jerusalem, if I forget you,
> may my right hand wither!
>
> May I never speak again,
> if I forget you!
> If I do not count Jerusalem
> the greatest of my joys!
> (Ps 137: 1-6)

The fall of Israel and Judah was a death blow to those who relied on political power to attain the kingdom promised by God. The *anawim*, on the other hand, discovered that God continued to walk

with his people in a foreign land. Their faith was
purified by the exile. They found God in the
wilderness. Zephaniah describes this process of
purification in these words: "When that day
comes you need feel no shame for all the misdeeds
you have committed against me, for I will remove
your proud boasters from your midst; I will leave a
humble and lowly people, and those who are left in
Israel will seek refuge in the name of Yahweh"
(Zp 3:11-12).

In the faithfulness of the *anawim* the spirituality
of the passover was reborn. The exile became a
journey of trust in Yahweh. Isaiah envisioned the
return from exile as a new exodus. God will lead
his people home in a new act of liberation. The
desert will bloom with life and "a highway will be
there called the holy way; no one unclean may
pass over it, no fools go astray on it. No lion will be
there, no beast of prey go up to be met upon it.
It is for those with a journey to make, and on it the
redeemed will walk. Those whom the Lord has
ransomed will return and enter Zion singing,
crowned with everlasting joy; they will meet with
joy and gladness, sorrow and mourning will flee"
(Is 35:8-10, NAB).

The *anawim* not only rediscovered the desert
covenant; they also brought about an essential
development in paschal spirituality. The quality of
their trust is revealed in their faithfulness to God
and in the courage with which they faced suffering. But their most important contribution to the
history of spirituality was the sense of *interiority*

with which they lived their relationship with God.
The true exodus is the inward journey of faith. The
real desert is the mountains and valleys of the
soul, the wilderness of the heart. The journey
toward freedom demands a transformation of
one's inner self.

The Servant of God and the Inward Journey

In the writings of the prophet Isaiah a mysterious figure appears who responds to God's call
with unconditional love. He is known as "the
suffering servant of Yahweh." We find a sensitive
and moving description of his faithfulness in four
lyrical songs which depict the ideal disciple of
Yahweh (cf Is 42:1-7; 49:1-9; 50:4-9; 52:13-53:12).

There are two ways in which we might understand the role of the Isaiahan servant figure: 1) as
the high point of Old Testament spirituality; and 2)
as the promise of the Servant who is to come.

From the perspective of the Old Testament, the
suffering servant is the ideal image of the people
of God. He is the corporate personality of Israel.
"You, Israel, my servant, Jacob whom I brought
from the confines of the earth and called from the
ends of the world; you to whom I said, 'You are my
servant, I have chosen you, not rejected you,' do
not be afraid, for I am with you; stop being
anxious and watchful, for I am your God. I give
you strength, I bring you help, I uphold you with
my victorious right hand" (Is 41:8-10).

In the countenance of the servant we can see
the pain and suffering of all the *habiru* who have

ever lived. He is the outcast, the rejected one, the man of sorrows (Is 53:2-3).

In his faithful response to Yahweh he is also the ideal figure of the *anawim*. He is the humble servant of the Lord who takes the sins and suffering of others upon himself. "Ours were the sufferings he bore, ours the sorrows he carried. But we, we thought of him as someone punished, struck by God, and brought low. Yet he was pierced through for our faults, crushed for our sins. On him lies a punishment that brings us peace, and through his wounds we are healed" (Is 53:4-5).

The servant of the Lord has interiorized the exodus journey. He is a pilgrim of trust, an image of the faithful remnant. His passover journey is the transformation of his inner self through faith and suffering. "The Lord has given me a disciple's tongue. So that I may know how to reply to the wearied, he provides me with speech. Each morning he wakes me to hear, to listen like a disciple. The Lord Yahweh has opened my ear. For my part, I made no resistance, neither did I turn away. I offered my back to those who struck me, my cheeks to those who tore at my beard; I did not cover my face against insult and spittle" (Is 50:4-6).

The second way of understanding the servant figure is to see in him a vision of the future. The qualities of the servant sum up the richest moral values of the desert covenant. In him the Old Testament spirituality of the Exodus reaches its high point. In the end, however, the Isaiahan model is only an *ideal* figure. The suffering servant did not actually live in the community of Israel. His faith and spirituality went beyond the tradition of the *habiru* and the *anawim*. He was the expression of a hope and a vision. He was the promise of a Servant who was still to come. He was an icon of Jesus.

Jesus: Fulfillment of Exodus Spirituality

When the Servant comes he reveals himself through the *habiru*. He receives his human life from Mary, the highly favored daughter of God's *anawim* (Lk 1:29-38). He is born in the presence of a humble carpenter and the creatures of the earth. He is seen first by shepherds. The Servant pitches his tent with the "lowly ones" who watch in the night; Joseph in his dreams, Mary in her faith, the shepherds with their flocks, Anna and Simeon in their old age. He comes to live with pilgrims and wayfarers: Mary on her way through the hill country to be with Elizabeth, Joseph leading the way toward Bethlehem, John the Baptist in the Judean desert.

The Servant is born among those who walk the wilderness road and who stand before God in trust.

The Servant comes to those who choose to watch things grow.

Chapter Seven

I GO TO THE FATHER

Jesus: The Way

". . . he resolutely took the road for Jerusalem"
(Lk 9:52)

The Journey of the Shepherd

When the scribes and pharisees complained that Jesus "welcomed sinners and ate with them" (Lk 15:3), Jesus asked them this question: "What man among you with a hundred sheep, losing one, would not leave the ninety-nine in the wilderness and go after the missing one till he found it? And when he found it, would he not joyfully take it on his shoulders and then, when he got home, call together his friends and neighbors? 'Rejoice with me,' he would say 'I have found my sheep that was lost.' In the same way, I tell you, there will be more rejoicing in heaven over one repentant sinner than over ninety-nine virtuous men who have no need of repentance" (Lk 15:4-7).

The parable of the lost sheep can appear to be a simple illustration of God's loving care for sinners. It can be given a comfortable interpretation that permits us to remain spectators rather than participants in the story. We can easily see ourselves among the ninety-nine as Jesus goes in search of the stray. We are content to picture Jesus carrying the sinner back to the reconciling experience of community and of forgiveness. We often think of redemption as someone else's need.

Cyril of Alexandria, one of the early fathers of the Church, gives a different interpretation to this parable. In his view, the ninety-nine just are the members of the heavenly court, the angels who stand in adoration before the Father. The lost sheep is humanity. We are all in need of repentance, for we have strayed into the desert of brokenness and sin. We are all in need of God's loving forgiveness. Jesus is the shepherd who leaves the security of the heavenly kingdom and risks his life in the wilderness searching for humanity. When he finds us, he takes our burden on his shoulders and carries us back to the community of heaven.

St. Paul also interpreted redemption as a saving journey in which Jesus entered the dark underworld of sin and brought humanity back to the Father. When he explains the meaning of Christ's resurrection and the gift of the Spirit, Paul quotes from Psalm 68: "When he ascended to the height, he captured prisoners, he gave gifts to men" (Ep 4:8). Paul then adds this interpretive note: "When it says, 'he ascended,' what does it mean if not that he descended right down to the lower regions of the earth? The one who rose higher than all the heavens to fill all things is none other than the one who descended" (Ep 4:9-10).

Jesus himself spoke of his life as a journey. During his last conversation with his disciples, Jesus tells them: "I came from the Father and have

come into the world and now I leave the world to
go to the Father" (Jn 16:28).

In all of these instances, Jesus' life is pictured as
a journey through struggle and death to new life.
Redemption is a passover. Salvation is the new
and final exodus. From the moment of the incarnation until his glorification at the right hand of
the Father, there is one mystery which is unfolding
in Jesus' life. It is the inward journey of trust in his
Father, the transformation of his life through love.
It is the pasch of the Lord.

The Journey of the Hero

The four gospels are the account of the saving
journey through which Christ leads us back to the
Father. They describe a real person—Jesus, the
son of Mary and the Son of God, who entered
human history and redeemed us by his life, death
and resurrection. In this sense, the gospels are
history. They record the most important of all
facts, namely, that we are saved and that there
is hope.

But the gospels are also literature. They express
the saving act of Jesus in human language. They
give words to our deepest feelings about life. They
describe the life and person of Jesus in terms of
the universal dream of salvation that is found in
all cultures and in all literature. If we approach
the gospels as an expression of human experience,
they can help enliven our faith. They can put us
into touch with life as a personal quest.

The theme of the quest is basic to all literature. We find the story of the hero and his journey in all cultures and in all historical epochs. We read it in the great epics of Greece and Rome; we hear it in the poetry of the Sumerians and in the creation stories of the North American Indians. From Gilgamesh to Dante, from Odysseus to Billy Budd, the human spirit is portrayed as a quest for life and meaning.

What is the significance of this quest? What is the role of the hero in relationship to the paschal mystery?

A hero is someone who goes someplace where no one else has ever been. His quest involves a journey into an unknown land to find the secret of immortality or to slay the dark forces of evil. The outward adventure in turn reflects an odyssey of the spirit through which the hero explores the wilderness of his own selfhood. In this sense, we are all heroes. No one else can go where we must go. No one else can wrestle with our freedom and our dreams for us. Others can love us and care for us. They can be our companions and our friends. Another can even be our saviour and our redeemer. But no one else can hope for us or love for us or believe for us. That is the unique gift and burden of each person. It is what makes us human. It is what gives us the capacity of being heroes.

The journey of the hero in literature is the communal expression of our personal search for

meaning. "Dreams are private myths," writes
Freud, "and myths are public dreams." Our
dreams, when we are aware of them and reflect
on them, reveal a pattern of quest. Sometimes we
are seeking to fulfill our needs and desires. At
other times we are fleeing from the dark shadows
and forms of our fears. Our lives, even in their
unconscious expression, reveal themselves as a
quest for meaning and fulfillment.

Myths are more than fanciful stories. They are
the communal expression of the most basic truths
in the human condition. Myths create images in
which we can understand our quest for salvation.
Myths are public dreams. They are a record of the
human spirit straining to transcend itself. The
hero is the symbol of our personal consciousness,
the expression of our search for ultimate meaning.

From the perspective of faith, the stories of
quest are more than an expression of a cultural
value. They are more than a national dream. They
are more than literature or psychological symbols
of human consciousness. They are expressions of
our search for God. Myths lead us to the edge of
faith. They articulate the beginnings of a spirituality.

The Stages of the Journey

In recent studies of comparative literature,
there has emerged what some authors describe as
the "monomyth." This represents a common pattern in the journey of the hero in various cultures.
Joseph Campbell describes three stages in the

hero's journey: (1) separation (2) initiation (3) return.

First, there is the experience of separation. This stage refers to the initial break one makes with security. This occurs for each of us at the moment of birth. It can occur again each time we experience a turning point in our lives.

"Home," says T. S. Eliot, "is where one starts from." In the beginning is the break, the leap forward toward life. In order for the hero to discover his identity, he must leave home. He must become uprooted. At this stage, the hero is often portrayed as a naked youth standing at the edge of his own mystery.

At various times in our lives, we must decide whether to set out into the unknown or to cling to the secure surroundings of the past. Sometimes we do not seem to have a choice. We are thrust into a new situation without warning and without consultation. However, the most fundamental choice remains even in these circumstances. We must decide upon our inner attitude toward life regardless of the circumstances in which we find ourselves.

This initial leap toward life involves our experience of plunging inward and backward; backward, as it were, in time; inward, into the depth of our own psyche. In dreams this is often experienced as the sensation of falling. Our support system is gone. We are floating on the turbulent sea of our own freedom.

The second stage of the hero's journey is that of

initiation. In our culture we have a popularized notion of initiation that easily obscures its deeper meaning. We associate it with the difficult and often humiliating experiences that a prospective member must undergo in order to become part of a group. There is a kernel of truth in this view, but we must look beneath the surface to discover its true significance.

Initiation comes from the Latin, in-itia, which means, "a going into," "an entering." It refers to the encounter with the dark forces of evil in our lives. The hero enters into the world of darkness and engages in battle with the powers that threaten human life and meaning. The initiates in the ancient mystery cults often took part in a ceremony in which they literally closed their eyes in a gesture of letting go and leaping into the unknown to struggle with death and darkness.

Christian baptism is the sacrament of initiation in this same sense. We become a member of the risen community only by entering the waters of death.

Today we sometimes use the phrase, "to take the plunge." This describes the same meaning as the original idea of initiation. This stage of the journey encompasses all the moments of struggle in our lives. It can refer to the anxiety we experience as we begin our first job. It is present when we risk everything by pursuing a new career. It is part of the awesome decision to marry or the agonizing choice to break off a relationship. More than that, it describes the lifelong struggle to live with our fears and to accept our limitations, the willingness to enter the dark spaces of our solitude and to face there the reality of our own death.

This struggle for life takes place in a setting of mystery and shadow. The image that is most frequently associated with this phase of the journey is that of *water*. We are born with a fascination for water. In our dreams it is frequently a symbol of our fears and of our dread of the unknown. Like other primordial elements, water conveys a sense of mystery and of ambiguity. Water gives life and refreshes us, but it can also threaten and destroy us. The ancient world looked upon the depth of the sea as the dwelling place of evil.

The hero must plunge into the dark sea and struggle with the unnamed forces that lurk there. The ensuing battle frequently ends in what appears to be the defeat and even the death of the hero. But the journey does not end there. Something dies in order that something deeper might be reborn. The hero turns and begins the long journey home.

The last stage of the journey is the return of the hero. No matter how intense the struggle or how devastating the defeat, human consciousness points toward rebirth. The struggle with chaos ends in a purifying and integrating experience that renews and transforms the hero. The journey has put him in touch with his identity. He may never bring back the prize for which he originally set out, but he himself returns a new person. Gilgamesh failed to bring back the plant of immortality, but he came back to Uruk as a mature man who had stretched his humanity to the limit. After his return he walked in the quiet acceptance of his human limitations. He knew that he was mortal. He had become a man.

The journey ends with the celebration of homecoming. Purified by struggle, the hero returns to celebrate a feast with his community. It is a feast of reunion and triumph. The cycle of human adventure has run its course.

The Mythic Journey and the Christian Passover

The monomyth can be understood as a description of every person's journey toward wholeness. It expresses in literary form the growth pattern of mystics and artists, of schizophrenics and saints. It is an account of the peak experiences and turning points in our search for God and for ourselves.

The myths of world literature are significant expressions of our human search for meaning. Because they touch our depths, they also touch our faith. Before God spoke to Abraham or Isaac or Jacob; before he spoke through the prophets, he first spoke through the beauty of creation and the mystery of human experience. Myths are one of the ways in which God speaks to us. They unveil the yearning of our hearts for salvation. They give words to our hunger for the divine.

It is not surprising that the paschal mystery of Christianity shares many things in common with the great myths and religions of humanity. But there are some significant differences. The subject matter and the reality of the Christian gospel go far beyond any human search for salvation. Jesus is more than a literary expression of our view of life. He is a living person. He is the revelation of the Father's love. He is truth in human flesh. His journey is more than a cultural model. It is a real exodus, a life lived in the real world of stables and dusty roads, lakeshores and fishing boats, lonely deserts and clamoring crowds. The journey of Jesus led him to an upper room, to a garden, and to a hill named Golgotha.

When John wrote to his fellow Christians, he wanted to share with them his sense of the reality of Jesus. He wanted to reassure them that he was not speaking of a phantom or of a mythic hero. He begins his letter with these words: "Something which has existed since the beginning, that we have heard, and we have seen with our own eyes; that we have watched and touched with our hands: the Word, who is life—this is our subject" (I Jn 1:1).

It is both helpful and challenging for us to view Jesus' life as fulfilling and perfecting the poetic journeys of human experience. As Christians we believe that Jesus is not only divine. We believe that he is the most integrated human person who ever lived. His life is a passover toward eternal life. His journey is an exodus toward the Father.

If we choose to follow him today, we must explore the lines and roads, the hills and valleys of his personal journey.

Jesus: The Servant-Hero of Humanity

The journey of Jesus is given poetic expression in an early Christian hymn which St. Paul incorporates as part of his letter to the Philippians: "In your minds you must be the same as Christ Jesus:

> His state was divine,
> yet he did not cling
> to his equality with God
> but emptied himself
> to assume the condition of a slave,
> and became as all men are;
> he was humbler yet,
> even to accepting death,
> death on a cross.
> But God raised him high
> and gave him the name
> which is above all other names
> so that all beings
> in the heavens, on earth and in the underworld,
> should bend the knee at the name of Jesus
> and that every tongue should acclaim
> Jesus Christ as Lord,
> to the glory of God the Father."
>
> (Ph 2:5-11)

This hymn summarizes the most important stages of the new exodus which Jesus accomplished in his life. There is a remarkable similarity between these stages of Christ's passover and the phases of the mythic hero's journey.

First, the hymn speaks of the *separation* of the Word of God from the heavenly community. Jesus does not cling to divinity but empties himself. This is in contrast to Adam and Eve and the rest of humanity who grasp at divinity in an attempt to "become like gods" (Gn 3:5). Jesus chooses to let go of security and become homeless for the sake of redeeming the human community.

The stage of *initiation* is described in terms of Jesus entering into the human condition. He sets out to plumb the depths of the human experience by assuming the status of a slave and by facing the painful and humiliating death on a cross.

Finally, the hymn sings of Christ's triumphal *return* in glory. The Servant breaks the bonds of death, and, rising victoriously from the dead, ascends to the right hand of the Father.

Jesus is the hero of humanity. He goes where no one else has ever been—into the darkest waters of human life to conquer death and lead humanity toward eternal life. His journey goes beyond the hungers of human consciousness. It transcends the world of dream and myth. It is more than poetry. The journey of Jesus is a real event that unfolds in the daylight of freedom and in the dark night of suffering. In the life of Jesus, as in the exodus of old, myth becomes history. Redemption is no longer a futile dream or a cosmic ritual of nature. The mythic journey has been transformed into the Way.

The Pasch of the Lord

There is one gospel, one "good news" which announces the salvation won for us by Christ. The evangelists simply develop four different perspectives on the meaning of this saving event. In all four versions there is a common theme: Jesus' life is portrayed as the new passover, the final exodus of humanity toward the promised kingdom.

Matthew, writing to Jewish converts, describes Jesus as the new Moses. From the mountainside, Jesus instructs the New Israel and invites them to enter into a deeper covenant with his Father. He gives them the new law of love. He seals the new covenant in his healing mission and, ultimately, through the shedding of his blood.

Mark places Jesus in the Isaiahan tradition of the suffering servant of Yahweh. Jesus is the "last of the just," the faithful member of the *anawim*, who takes upon himself the sins of the people. He reconciles humanity with the Father.

In the gospel of Luke, the major part of Jesus' public life takes place in the context of a journey (cf. Lk 9:51-18:14). The journey begins with these significant words: "Now as the time drew near for him to be taken up to heaven [literally, "his passage to heaven"], he resolutely took the road for Jerusalem and sent messengers on ahead of him" (Lk 9:51-52). Luke departs from the historical sequence given by Mark and assembles the basic sources of the gospel tradition with the literary framework of a journey to Jerusalem. In doing so, Luke is developing a theology of Christ's life as the new and final passover.

Finally, in the gospel of John, the paschal mystery appears in still another perspective. John sees Jesus as the new paschal lamb whose blood redeems humanity (cf Jn 1:29). The major events of Jesus' public life center around three different passover feasts. John's account reaches its climax when Jesus takes the place of the traditional paschal lamb by his death on the cross (Jn 19:36-37). The entire gospel is pervaded by the theme of the Christian Passover replacing the Jewish Passover.

With this background, we can now reflect on the stages of Jesus' paschal journey as they unfold in the mystery of his life.[1]

Separation: The Homelessness of Christ

There is an ancient Advent hymn in which the Church quotes from the book of Wisdom to describe the incarnation of Christ: "When peaceful silence lay over all, and night had run the half of her swift course, down from the heavens, from the royal throne, leapt your all-powerful Word" (Ws 18:14-15).

Although the passage is taken out of context, the intent of the hymn is clear. It is an antiphon which portrays the "leap" of the Word of God into human life. It describes the separation of the Word from the heavenly community in order that

he might begin the saving journey which will bring
humanity back to God. The Son leaves the light of
the heavenly kingdom and enters the darkness of a
sinful world. He experiences the homelessness of
the human condition.

Jesus is born of a lowly Jewish maiden. His
stepfather is a humble carpenter. Together, they
are *anawim* who trust in the loving goodness of
Yahweh. They are *habiru,* members of an oppressed people who must report for a census in
their native village. Jesus is born during a journey
and his life is framed in homelessness. He is born
in a cave for animals. He is buried in a stranger's
tomb. His life takes the form of a passage, a
continuous setting forth, a pilgrimage in search of
life.

While still an infant, Jesus is taken into Egypt; at
twelve, he is "lost" in the temple; at thirty, he
makes the desert journey; and at thirty-three, he
walks into a garden to wrestle with death. Jesus
tells those who wish to follow him that discipleship
will demand a spirit of pilgrimage. "Foxes have
holes and the birds of the air have nests, but the
Son of man has nowhere to lay his head" (Lk 9:58).

In the early morning, Jesus seeks the solitude of
the desert to pray. His disciples seek him out to tell
him that "everyone is looking for you" (Mk 1:37).
Jesus' response is a summary of his life and
mission: "Let us go elsewhere, to the neighboring
country towns, so that I can preach there too,
because that is why I came" (Mk 1:38).

The prologue of John's gospel begins with these simple words:

> In the beginning was the Word;
> The Word was with God
> and the Word was God.

The Word was with God. This description seems to convey a sense of rest and of divine immutability. But the Greek term that is translated as "with" in this phrase is *pros*. This is an active word, not a static one. *Pros* can best be translated as *towards* God. At the beginning of his gospel, John gives us a theology of pilgrimage. From all eternity the Word has been in a relationship of active response to the Father. The Word has been *towards* God. In the mystery of the incarnation, the Word becomes flesh and dwells with us. His response of love to the Father takes the form of human pilgrimage. The inward stance of his life is the same as that of the eternal Word. He continues to be totally dedicated to his Father's will. Jesus' life was lived "towards the Father." His life was a journey toward ever deeper union with the God from whom he had come. "I came from the Father and have come into the world and now I leave the world to go to the Father" (Jn 16:28).

Initiation: The Man of Sorrows

The struggle with evil in Jesus' life is not limited to his passion and death. He wrestles the dark

forces of sin from the very beginning of his life.
The infancy narratives introduce the theme of
suffering as they describe the persecution of the
Jews by Herod, the death of the innocents, and the
flight into Egypt.

The gospels picture the world as under the
dominion of Satan. Disease, divisions, prejudice
and hatred are signs of the pervading presence of
sin. Christ's entry into the world is the beginning
of a struggle for life in a world dominated by
death.

Jesus begins his public life at the Jordan with
John the Baptist. He plunges into the dark waters
as a symbol that the decisive encounter between
life and death is about to begin. Jesus comes out of
the waters filled with the Spirit and committed to
his mission to be the suffering servant.

Immediately he goes into the desert and engages
in combat with Satan. Jesus relives the journey
and the temptations of his ancestors in the desert.
Unlike them, he does not turn aside from the
wilderness that awaits him. He is faithful to the
call to be the obedient servant of the Father.

The struggle with darkness continues in his
public ministry. Jesus confronts the presence of
evil in the blind, the mute, the deaf, the lame, the
lepers and the possessed. Ironically, it is the
unclean spirits that first acknowledge the presence of God acting in Jesus. "What do you want
with us, Jesus of Nazareth? Have you come to
destroy us? I know who you are: the Holy One of
God" (Mk 1:24). The world of darkness under-

stands better than humanity that the decisive battle is now being fought.

The only person who realizes this with greater clarity is Jesus himself. He knows that the new exodus can only be accomplished through suffering. The wilderness road is a way of pain. At first he speaks of suffering as any rabbi might. He teaches his followers that pain is an essential part of growth in discipleship. But as the hatred of the Jewish leaders increases and as the opposition of the crowds grows in intensity, Jesus speaks in more personal terms. He speaks about *his* suffering and *his* death. "Now we are going up to Jerusalem, and everything that is written by the prophets about the Son of Man is to come true. For he will be handed over to the pagans and will be mocked, maltreated and spat on, and when they have scourged him they will put him to death; and on the third day he will rise again" (Lk 18:31-33). In this passage, Jesus is no longer speaking as a rabbi, but as the suffering servant, who knows that his hour is near.

From then on Jesus moves toward his passion and death with freedom and conviction. It becomes the consuming desire of his life. "I have come to bring fire to the earth," he tells his followers, "and how I wish it were blazing already. There is a baptism I must still receive, and how great is my distress till it is over" (Lk 12:49-50). Jesus sees his journey as a "baptism," a plunging, a passage through dark waters toward life. He expresses this same urgent desire to complete the journey

when he speaks to his disciples at the last supper:
"I have longed to eat this passover with you before
I suffer, because, I tell you, I shall not eat it again
until it is fulfilled in the kingdom of God" (Lk
22:15-16).

Jesus had gathered his friends together for the
last time. "It was before the festival of the Passover, and Jesus knew that the hour had come for
him to pass from this world to the Father. He had
always loved those who were his own in this
world, but now he showed how perfect his love
was" (Jn 13:1). Together they celebrated the
paschal meal. In a moving gesture of love, Jesus
transformed the ancient meal into a new feast. He
shared the bread and the cup. He gave his body
and his blood for the life of humanity. The age-old
feast became the sacrament of the New Covenant.
The new and eternal passover had begun.

Immediately after the meal Jesus went out into
the night. The final struggle with darkness began.
The synoptics simply say that Jesus went with his
disciples to a plot of land, but John specifically
describes it as a garden. Jesus crossed the Kedron
Valley and entered Gethsemane. It is an echo of
the mythic hero crossing the dark waters to enter
the garden of life. For Jesus, however, the garden
of Eden had become a place of agony. There Jesus
faced the fears of his own heart, and then he
walked toward death.

Return: The Forerunner of Humanity

In John's gospel, the death and resurrection of
Jesus are not seen as two separate events, but as

two phases of Christ's paschal journey to the
Father. During his public ministry, Jesus spoke of
his death and resurrection as a passage through
suffering to glory. Specifically, he spoke of being
"lifted up." In using this phrase Jesus was referring both to his agony on the cross and to the
glory of his resurrection. When the Jews ques-
tioned him about his relationship with his Father,
Jesus told them: "When you have *lifted up* the Son
of Man, then you will know that I am He and that I
do nothing of myself: what the Father has taught
me is what I preach; he who sent me is with me,
and has not left me to myself, for I always do what
pleases him" (Jn 8:28-29).

In his last encounter with the crowds, Jesus
repeats this theme: "When I am *lifted up* from
the earth, I shall draw all men to myself"
(Jn 12:32).

Jesus' words contain an important truth for
those of us who follow him. The Christian passover
journey does not isolate sorrow and joy, suffering
and glorification. The pasch of the Lord is one
journey toward life. Christianity is good news
precisely because it challenges us to see light in
the darkness and to trust the promise of life in the
face of death. Jesus is lifted up both in agony and
in glory. He is at once Servant and Lord, Lamb
and Shepherd. After his resurrection Jesus carries his wounds in his risen body as a sign of
recognition and as a symbol of victory. Because he
did not hesitate to embrace the mystery of death,
he is able to draw to himself all of life.

"Go and find the brothers, and tell them: I am

ascending to my Father and to your Father, to my God and to your God" (Jn 20:17). These are the directions that Jesus gives to Mary Magdalene in the garden after his resurrection. They are words of victory and of hope. The Servant-Hero returns now to the heavenly kingdom in triumph.

But he does not return alone. Jesus is the "first-born of many brothers and sisters" (Col 1:18; Rv 1:5). He has become the way to life for all who follow him. The pasch of the Lord is the journey of every Christian.

This is the same message that the author of the letter to the Hebrews wants to share with his fellow Christians. He writes to reassure the Jewish converts that Jesus is the fulfillment of the ancient longing for a saviour. He is the high priest who shares all our weaknesses except sin. He has made the human journey to its depths. He has embraced life in all its mystery and ambiguity. He has broken through "the veil" (Heb 6:20) and opened a way to the Father.

The author of Hebrews encourages the new Christians to "take a firm grip on the hope" that is held out to them. What reason is there to hope? The "anchor" of our hope is that Jesus is the prodromos—"the forerunner" (Heb 6:20), who goes on ahead to prepare a place for us. Jesus is the pilgrim who has become the road. He is the wayfarer who has become the Way. Jesus is our passover to life.

Chapter Eight

FOLLOWERS OF THE WAY

The New Pilgrim People

Home is where one starts from. As we grow older
The world becomes stranger, the pattern more complicated
Of dead and living. Not the intense moment
Isolated, with no before and after,
But a lifetime burning in every moment . . .

> T. S. Eliot
> "East Coker"

Stephen: The Emergence of a Pattern

A man named Stephen had been sentenced to die. Like fire on the edge of the desert, the word spread through Jerusalem. The marketplace came alive with rumors. Children ran in the streets. The curious came to watch.

It had happened so quickly. Stephen, a deacon in the small sect that believed in Jesus of Nazareth, had been preaching the New Way near the temple. In anger, a group of Jews seized him and took him before the Sanhedrin. With the help of false witnesses, and in angry reaction to Stephen's outspoken words, the council arrived at a hasty decision. Stephen was condemned to death for blasphemy. In accordance with the ancient law, he was taken outside the city to be stoned.

The frenzy of the crowd grew until it could no longer be contained. As they began to hurl stones at him, Stephen prayed, "Lord Jesus, receive my spirit" (Ac 7:59). He fell to his knees under the blows of the rocks and said, "Lord, do not hold this sin against them" (Ac 7:60).

Then it was finished. Silence came over the crowd as they turned to walk away, and in the silence something was born. The blood of a man soaked the earth and a seed was sown. A power was released. All the stones in the world could not stop its energy from spreading, like waves of light, across the land.

We do not remember the accusers or the false witnesses of that day. We have forgotten the judges and the crowds. But we will forever remember Stephen as the first martyr of Christianity.

The literal translation of martyr is "witness." Martyrs are people who have seen something significant in life. They are more than observers or curious bystanders. They are witnesses who have become involved in what they have seen. They have been pulled from the edge of the crowd toward the center of life.

Martyrs speak their testimony in the language of courage and commitment. They give an account of what they have seen from the inside of life—through their vision and their actions. They live what they have witnessed. They share what they have seen.

What led Stephen to give this kind of witness? What did he see?

He saw that Jesus of Nazareth had created a

sacred way through the darkness of human existence. He understood to what extent Jesus had
gone where no one else had ever been. Stephen
saw that Jesus had broken through to new life and
he wished to be a witness to this resurrection. "I
can see heaven thrown open," he told the Sanhedrin,"and the Son of Man standing at the right
hand of God" (Ac 7:56).

Stephen saw that Jesus was the way to life. But
he saw more than that. He also understood the
personal implications of Christ's paschal journey.
He realized that Jesus not only made the journey
for us, but he also makes it *with* us and *in* us. This
is the most important realization of all. The new
exodus of the Lord is self-involving. It calls
observers to become witnesses. It transforms
seekers into disciples. Jesus is not an isolated
redeemer who saves humanity by a divine decree;
he is a *homo viator*, a wayfarer among pilgrims,
who invites them to follow him. He is "the first-
born of many brothers and sisters." He is the forerunner of humanity.

Stephen is Christianity's first martyr because he
is the first witness to relive the pattern of Christ's
journey to the full. There is more involved in
martyrdom than shedding one's blood. What
matters most is the inward vision which led
Stephen to this radical commitment.

St. Luke is careful to point out the similarity
between Stephen's death and the passion of Jesus.
Like Jesus, Stephen encounters the opposition of
the Jewish leaders. He is taken to trial. There are

the false witnesses and the same accusations of
blasphemy. Stephen stands before his accusers
with the same inner calm that filled Jesus. He is a
profile of peace in a crowd of violence. He dies in
prayer, forgiving his executioners in the same
words with which Jesus had forgiven his. He
commends his soul to Jesus, as once the Lord had
commended his spirit to the Father.

What does it mean to be a disciple of Jesus? The
pattern which emerges in Stephen's life and death
gives us a basis for answering this question.
Christianity is more than a philosophy of life or a
collection of doctrines. It is more than a moral
code or a series of rites for worship. Christianity
is, first of all, a personal journey. It is a way of
living. It is not as concerned about explaining life
as it is committed to living it fully and deeply.
Christianity is the choice to follow Jesus in his life
of service and of healing, his passover journey of
love.

This is the conviction that permeated the life of
Stephen. It moved him to make the paschal
journey of Christ a reality in his own life. It is the
reason why the early Christians were first called
"Followers of the Way." Christians are those who
follow the Lord in the new exodus toward eternal
life. Stephen traced out the image and the reality
of the Lord's pasch in his own flesh. He was the
beginning of a pattern, an ever-expanding circle
of those who would become companions in the
paschal mystery.

"The blood of martyrs is a seed." This hopeful

phrase was heard often on the lips of the early
Christians. It proved to be a vision of the world
that was still to come. The blood soaked into the
ground. The seed fell into the soil of history. It is
still growing in our lives.

Paul: The Development of a Spirituality

A young man stood at the edge of the crowd. He
watched silently, his eyes burning with determination. He threw no rocks, but the lines on his
face were tense with excitement and conviction.
He clearly approved of what was happening
before him.

"The witnesses put down their clothes at the
feet of a young man named Saul" (Ac 7:58). In
these simple words, Luke introduces the central
figure of the Acts of the Apostles. The martrydom
of Stephen is a prelude to the story of Saul, the
Pharisee. He stands at the edge of the crowd as
though he were waiting at the perimeter of his
own life. In the plan of God, he is about to be
pulled from the periphery of history into the center
of the passover mystery. The pattern of discipleship which Stephen enfleshed in his life widens to
include the life and search of Paul. It deepens to
become a spirituality of the paschal mystery.

The conversion of Saul is one of the most
familiar and dramatic stories in New Testament
literature. Saul was on his way to Damascus, "still
breathing threats to slaughter the Lord's disciples" (Ac 9:1), when he encountered the risen
Christ. Saul fell to the ground in a blinding flash of

light. He heard a voice saying, "Saul, Saul, why
are you persecuting me?" "Who are you, Lord?" he
asked, and the voice answered, "I am Jesus, and
you are persecuting me. Get up now and go into
the city, and you will be told what you have to do"
(Ac 9:4-5).

This meeting on the Damascus road was as
decisive in the life of Saul as the Exodus event had
been in the life of the Jewish people. Whatever the
distance from Jerusalem to Damascus, it could not
compare with the long journey of the spirit that
began in Saul at that moment. Saul, the proud
Israelite, who had dedicated his life to the law and
the purification of Jewish religion, suddenly found
himself blind and helpless, choking in the dust of
his own life. It is a long way from Saul of Tarsus to
Paul the Apostle, but the journey began there on
the Damascus road. Saul, the Pharisee, died in the
dust and darkness of that noon. "Get up now and
go . . ." It is a call to a new birth. It is an invitation
to live the paschal journey of Christ.

The man who stood at the edge of the crowd was
drawn irresistibly toward the Way which he had
once tried to destroy. The man who stood at the
edge of the crowd groped his way toward Damascus and toward a new life. The persecutor had
become a follower. He began with stumbling
steps, but even then, in his confusion, his groping
was already a journey. He had begun to walk the
wilderness road of death and resurrection.

"I myself will show him how much he himself
must suffer for my name" (Ac 9:17). These were

the words with which the Lord characterized the
future life of Paul. In his ministry of preaching,
Paul identified his life with the paschal journey of
Jesus. He summarizes his life and mission as an
apostle in these moving words: "Always, wher-
ever we may be, we carry with us in our body the
death of Jesus, so that the life of Jesus, too, may
always be seen in our body. Indeed, while we are
still alive, we are consigned to our death every
day, for the sake of Jesus, so that in our mortal
flesh the life of Jesus, too, may be openly shown"
(II Cor 4:10-11).

The encounter with the risen Lord was the most
important experience in Paul's life. It was the
decisive event that enabled him to understand his
past and to shape his future in an entirely new
way. But it was only the beginning. Spiritual
rebirth is more than an event; it is a life process.
Paul spent the rest of his life living, preaching,
and sharing the light which had blinded him on the
road. He spent the rest of his life being born. Paul
claimed the title "apostle" because he had seen
the risen Lord. He accepted this office not out of
arrogance, but out of a sense of responsibility and
personal conviction. "I am the least of the apostles; in fact, since I persecuted the Church of God,
I hardly deserve the name apostle; but by God's
grace that is what I am, and the grace he gave me
has not been fruitless" (I Cor 15:9-10).

Paul may have been "born out of due time," but
his experience gave him the perspective and insight necessary to make him one of the most

significant figures in the growth of the early Church. It is Paul rather than the other apostles who develops a theology of Christian life. It is Paul who presents us with a spirituality of the paschal mystery. Paul follows the pattern that emerged with Stephen. He, too, became a witness to the resurrection. But Paul went beyond living the paschal mystery; he attempted to describe it and to preach it. He tried to tell us what it means to be a Follower of the Way.

Faith as a Journey

Paul was a wayfarer of the Spirit. After his conversion, he moved about the Mediterranean world in a spirit of urgency and pilgrimage. He formed communities of faith, and then moved on to preach the risen Christ in new places. He preached the gospel with the same intensity with which he had once persecuted the followers of the Way. He made tents and lived in them.

Understandably, Paul places the Christian life in the framework of pilgrimage. The experience of his own search for meaning permeates his theology and his letters. The theme of journey weaves its way through his preaching and his writing like sunlight on a cloudy day. It is always there, sometimes quietly behind the scene; sometimes openly in a burst of warmth and energy. Most of the words that St. Paul employs to describe the life of a Christian are words of movement. The Christian "walks," "runs," and "strains to go forward." "All the runners at the stadium are trying to win," he tells the Corinthians, "but only one of them gets the prize. You must run in the same way, meaning to win" (I Cor 9:24). He congratulates the Galatians by telling them that they "ran well" (5:7), and toward the end of his own life he says, "I have finished my course" (II Tim 4:7).

There is a sense of urgency about Paul's preaching and journeys. He speaks of "pressing on" and of moving toward the goal of complete identification with the Lord Jesus. Paul never forgot the words that he heard and felt that day on the road: "Get up now and go . . . ."

In Christ: Sharing the Paschal Mystery

Many spiritual writers have described the Christian life as though it were simply an ethical imitation of its founder. St. Paul makes it clear that following the Way is far more than copying the moral behavior of Jesus. The Christian journey of faith is an actual *participation* in the paschal journey of Christ.

Biblical scholars point out that one of the most frequently used phrases in Pauline theology are the words, "in Christ." The Paschal journey of Jesus is not merely imitated in the life of the Christian, it is lived in identity and communion with the Lord. The words of the risen Lord were burned into his memory: "Saul, Saul, why are you persecuting *me*?" Who is this presence who so closely identifies himself with his followers that he shares their sufferings and search? His conver-

sion left Paul with a profound awareness of the
intimate union which exists between the risen
Christ and those who follow him. Paul uses many
different images to convey the depth of this union.
Often he speaks of the Christian community as the
"Body of Christ." The parts of a body all share the
same life principle and the same process of
growth. Christ is the life principle of the Christian
community. His paschal journey is the pattern of
growth which the entire body shares.

Baptized into Christ

One of the clearest expressions of identity with
Christ's journey is found in Paul's theology of
baptism. Baptism means "plunging"—it is a word
of journey and of process. Cleansing and ritual
purification are only secondary connotations of
the word. The Jewish people had a practice of
baptizing converts who wished to join the Israelite
community. The rite was based on the conviction
that people can only share life in community if
they first experience the most important event in
the history of that people. As we have seen, the
exodus event was the decisive religious experience for Israel. If anyone wished to share Israel's
life of faith, they must, at least ritually, experience the passage through the dark waters to new
life. They must be "baptized"—plunged into the
waters—in order to achieve this intimate union of
life.

The baptism of John, which is characterized in
the gospels as a baptism of repentance, may have

shared some of this same emphasis on the meaning
of the exodus. John's baptism was more than a
ritual purification or a simple call to repentance.
It was a challenge to return to the desert covenant, an invitation to relive the exodus in the
personal response of faith.

With this background in Jewish spirituality,
Paul interprets the meaning of Christian baptism
in a similar fashion. The most important event in
Christian history is the new exodus which was
accomplished in the passover journey of Jesus. He
is *the Way*. If we choose to be followers of the
Way, we must experience this same decisive event
in our lives. We can only be "in Christ" if we
share his life experience. We must ritually celebrate and personally live out the paschal mystery
of the Lord. We must plunge into the dark waters
of death, and, leaving behind the old self, rise to a
new life.

Baptism is more than ritual imitation. It is a
sacramental *participation* in the pasch of the
Lord. It is an outward celebration of an inward
communion of life. It is a ritualization of a life
process that continues to unfold throughout our
lives.

With this background, Paul's familiar words
take on new and significant meaning: "You have
been taught that when we were baptized in Christ
Jesus we were baptized into his death; in other
words, when we were baptized we went into the
tomb with him and joined him in death, so that as
Christ was raised from the dead by the Father's

glory, we too might live a new life. If in union with Christ we have imitated his death, we shall also imitate him in his resurrection. We must realize that our former selves have been crucified with him to destroy this sinful body and to free us from the slavery of sin. When a man dies, of course, he has finished with sin. But we believe that having died with Christ we shall return to life with him: Christ, as we know, having been raised from the dead will never die again. Death has no power over him any more. When he died, he died, once for all, to sin, so his life now is life with God; and in that way, you too must consider yourselves to be dead to sin but alive for God in Christ Jesus" (Rm 6:5-11).

The Eucharist: Food for the Journey

Throughout his letters, Paul characterizes the Church as the new exodus community. Each of the local communities is a new passover people. The Christian passover is celebrated once a week rather than once a year. It is observed on the first day of the week, the day of resurrection. This day soon became known as the *dies domini*, the Day of the Lord. It was on this day that the disciples had first encountered the risen Lord and shared a meal with him.

Paul develops his theology of the Eucharist in the context of the ancient passover meal. Just as the ancient *habiru* were nourished by Yahweh in the desert, so the Christian is fed with the bread of

life in the Lord's supper. In the view of Paul, Jesus
is not only the new paschal lamb, he is also the
new unleavened bread. As we have seen, the
Jewish people removed all the old leaven from
their houses during the passover feast. They ate
only unleavened bread to remind themselves of the
haste with which they left Egypt. Unleavened
bread is bread for pilgrims.

Paul translates this ancient symbolism into new
meaning when he applies it to the Christian passover. Because Christians are united with the
sacrifice of the risen Lord and his eternal passover, they must remove the "old yeast," the leaven
of selfishness and sin. They must be nourished by
the unleavened bread of the risen Christ. "You
must know how even a small amount of yeast is
enough to leaven all the dough, so get rid of all the
old yeast, and make yourselves into a completely
new batch of bread, unleavened as you are meant
to be. Christ, our passover, has been sacrificed;
let us celebrate the feast, then, by getting rid of all
the old yeast of evil and wickedness, having only
the unleavened bread of sincerity and truth"
(I Cor 5:6-8).

The supper of the Lord strengthens the unity
which Christians have with Christ and with each
other. It celebrates their common destiny and
their shared journey toward the Father. "The
blessing-cup that we bless is a communion with
the blood of Christ, and the bread that we break is
a communion with the body of Christ. The fact that

there is only one loaf means that, though there are
many of us, we form a single body because we all
have a share in this one loaf" (I Cor 10:16-17).

To Live is Christ: The Mysticism of Paul

A spirituality is a vision of life. It gives expression to the search of the human heart as it
encounters the living God. Christian spirituality
is not a formula for ethical behavior; it is an expression of an inner process of transformation.
It articulates an experience that is at the center
of one's life.

Paul developed his spirituality of the paschal
mystery in the crucible of his own life. He
preached the risen Christ that he had encountered
on the road to Damascus. He described a spirituality that flowed from his own religious experience. He knew what it meant to die and rise again.
He lived the paschal mystery in his own flesh
before he began to preach it as a way of life.

In Paul's view, the Christian life has but one
goal: to follow Christ in his passover journey; to
become so united with him, that one experiences
identity with the risen Lord. The paschal journey
calls for the inward transformation of the self.
Paul speaks of three stages in this inner journey:
(1) justification (2) sanctification and (3) glorification.

(1) *Justification* is God's initial act of saving us
from our darkness and despair. It is the beginning
of the journey toward life. Justification is a total
gift from God. It is the unconditional acceptance of

our lives in Jesus. The Father calls us by name. He invites us to turn from our aimless wandering and become pilgrims with the Lord.

Until his conversion, Paul spent his life trying to justify himself by his dedicated adherence to the Jewish law. His conversion forced him to see with clarity that no amount of human effort can ever establish our own worthiness. It is God who makes us just. It is God who gives us holiness and the capacity to become fully ourselves.

The biblical concept of justice is not the same as that of the Greeks and the Romans. The Greeks thought of justice in terms of the equal distribution of rights or goods. They pictured it as an orderly balance between human beings. This kind of justice is expressed in the familiar symbol of the scales. The Hebrews approached justice differently. They saw it as a gift from God rather than a juridical balance between human beings. God justifies us when he gratuitously gives us a share in his life and holiness. God justifies us when he enables us to stand "upright" and to walk toward life. "The upright man finds life through faith" (Rm 1:17). God's justice cannot be earned by human effort; it can only be received in trust. Paul experienced justification when a loving Presence lifted him out of the dust of the road and said, "Get up now and go . . ." Justification is the beginning of the paschal journey.

(2) *Sanctification* is the inward growth that takes place between initial justification and final glorification. The major part of Christian life is

spent "on the way" that leads from God's gift to God's destiny. During this journey we are "led by the Spirit" (Rm 8:14), who transforms our lives into the image of the risen Lord. Sanctification is what happens to us when we are faithful followers of the Way. It is the long journey from Saul of Tarsus to Paul the Apostle. It is the groaning of the Spirit within us (Rm 8:26-27) as he finds words for our sighing and direction for our lives.

Paul describes this transformation of the self as a gradual divinization of our lives by the Holy Spirit. In his view, every Christian is called to a deep, mystical union with the risen Christ. Like Moses we encounter the Lord in the brightness of his presence. Unlike Moses, we no longer veil our faces before the living God. We encounter Christ face to face. We enter into a personal relationship of love with the Lord. "And we, with our unveiled faces reflecting like mirrors the brightness of the Lord, all grow brighter and brighter as we are turned into the image that we reflect; this is the work of the Lord who is Spirit" (II Cor 3:18).

We can only be "turned into the image that we reflect," if we participate fully in the new exodus of Christ. Death and resurrection are more than metaphors in Christian life; they are real experiences in the process of our sanctification. Something must die in us in order that Christ may live in us. "You must give up your old way of life," Paul tells the Ephesians, "you must put aside your old self which gets corrupted by illusory desires. Your mind must be renewed by a spiritual revolu-

tion so that you can put on the new self that has
been created in God's way, in the goodness and
holiness of truth" (Eph 4:22-24).

Paul identifies his life with Christ. His old,
pharisaical self has died. A new principle of life,
the presence of the Holy Spirit is at work within
him. "I have been crucified with Christ, and I live
now not with my own life, but with the life of
Christ who lives in me" (Gal 2:19-20).

St. Paul describes a vision of spirituality that
touches our deepest hunger for God. His vision is
rooted in a profound experience of mystical union
with Christ. In our age, when so many people
hunger for God, we often neglect the rich sources
of the Christian tradition. Many people have
turned to other religions and philosophies of life to
find what Christianity has always offered—a way
toward union with God. It is true that Paul's
language sometimes seems to parallel the ideas of
oriental, mystical thought. Zen Buddhism also
calls for the death of the outer, superficial self, so
that the divine spark within may emerge toward
life. But Paul's vision is an incarnational spirituality, rooted in the paschal mystery of Jesus,
and calling upon us to be witnesses in the marketplace of life. Paul's mysticism is not a withdrawal
from life, but a transformation of human experience into risen life.

(3) *Glorification* is the destiny of the Christian
life. The passover journey moves toward final
fulfillment. As we travel the road of self-denial
and faith, we walk in hope, for we trust in the

promise of everlasting life. The paschal mystery of
Christ is the model for the future. His resurrection
is the basis for Christian hope. Jesus, the forerunner of humanity, has already achieved eternal
glory. The Christian community still walks in the
dim light of faith, but its destiny will be the same
as Christ's.

Toward the end of his life Paul sat in prison in
Rome and reflected on the roads that he had
walked. He knew that he had moved from the
edge of the crowd to the center of life. He was
filled with a sense of gratitude. He saw a vision of
hope. From his confinement he wrote to the community at Philippi. His words provide us with a
summary of what it means to be a follower of the
Way: "Because of Christ, I have come to consider
all these advantages that I had as disadvantages.
Not only that, but I believe nothing can happen
that will outweigh the supreme advantage of
knowing Christ Jesus my Lord. For him I have
accepted the loss of everything, and I look on
everything as so much rubbish if only I can have
Christ and be given a place in him. I am no longer
trying for perfection by my own efforts, the perfection that comes through faith in Christ, and is
from God and based on faith. All I want is to know
Christ and the power of his resurrection and to
share his sufferings by reproducing the pattern of
his death. That is the way I can hope to take my
place in the resurrection of the dead. Not that I
have become perfect yet: I have not yet won, but I
am still running, trying to capture the prize for

which Christ Jesus captured me. I can assure you
my brothers, I am far from thinking that I have
already won. All I can say is that I forget the past
and strain ahead for what is still to come; I am
racing for the finish, for the prize to which God
calls us upwards to receive in Christ Jesus . . .
meanwhile, let us go forward on the road that has
brought us to where we are" (Phil 3:7-16).

Following the Way

Christianity is a way toward life. We describe
this way as "the paschal mystery," because it is a
call to share a journey and to make a passage
through death to new life.

The *habiru* followed this way in the wilderness.
The *anawim* lived it during the exile. The prophets
proclaimed it in the cities and preached it on the
edge of the desert.

Jesus brought the way to perfection through his
personal passover to new life. He is *the* Way.
Jesus invites humanity to come after him in the
quest for eternal life. He calls us to be Followers of
the Way.

Stephen and Paul and the other disciples expressed the Way in their preaching and in their
lives. They proclaimed it with their blood. The
blood soaked into the ground. The seed fell into the
soil of history. It is still growing in our lives.

Chapter Nine

TO DANCE, TO WEEP, TO JOURNEY TOWARD GOD
The Paschal Mystery Today

From Nothingness to God

In his novel, *St. Francis*, Nikos Kazantzakis sketches a joyfully human portrait of the disciple from Assisi. In one scene, Francis and his companions are singing through the streets of Rome, filled with the presence of God and the joy of the gospel. An astonished young noblewoman laughs at them and asks:

> " 'Where do you come from?'
> 'From nothingness, madam.'
> 'Where are you going?'
> 'To God. On the way between nothingness and
> God,
> we dance and weep.'
>
> The young woman was not laughing now. Her dress was open at the collar. Placing her right hand over her exposed throat, she sighed, 'Is this what we were born for?'
> 'Yes, madam: to dance, weep, and journey toward God.' "[1]

In his reply to the noblewoman, Francis has captured some of the rich meaning of the Christian life. He has put the paschal mystery into poetry. Christians are pilgrims who are on the way from nothingness to God. Along the way, they weep and they dance, they cry and they laugh, they die and they rise.

Weeping and dancing are a description of the human condition. They express the rhythm of our days and the cycles of our moods. They speak of the ebb and flow of our daily struggle to find meaning. If we were to view the sorrow and joy of our lives apart from our destiny, they might leave us empty and afraid. Weeping and dancing only make sense if we see them as part of our journey toward God. If life has a direction, it can carry its contradictions with hope. We need a vision of life to give meaning and shape to the flow of our experience. We need a spirituality to make sense out of the tears and laughter of the human journey.

There is a growing hunger for spiritual vision today. This desire arises from our personal search for meaning. It grows out of our quest for an authentic experience of contemplation.

The pace of our living has accelerated. The tempo of change is threatening to destroy our inwardness. Our lives are filled with plans and projects. There is work to be done at the office; there is housework waiting at home; the crops are in need of harvesting; the children have the flu; the holidays are coming.

We become so preoccupied with the needs and demands of the present that we lose a sense of perspective. We keep lists and meet deadlines. We mark our calendars and fill our lives with appointments. We approach the future with anx-

iety and carry the past with regret. We seldom
find time to view our lives as an integral experience. We neglect the vision. We lose touch with
the current of silence that flows within us. We
dance and we weep, but we appear to be puppets.
We forget that our lives are a journey from nothingness to God.

For all that, the spirit cannot be suppressed.
The restlessness persists. The noise that surrounds us cannot drown the silence within us. The
gatherings leave us lonely. The hunger for God
will not die. In glimpses and passing moments,
grace invades our lives.

We pause to look out the window before we go
to bed, and in the moonlight, we see shadows
across the snow. For a moment we study the
pattern of our lives. We see a direction. We touch
the silence and go to sleep.

We drive home in the rush hour traffic with our
minds still auditing the day. Our emotions are
tense and strained. Beyond the traffic and the
urban haze, the sun is setting. The sky is crim-
son—an unexpected gift of beauty. Without real-
izing it, we are praying.

Technology has not deadened our hunger for the
spirit; it has only made us more aware of ourselves and of our search for God. It has increased
our personal responsibility to create space for
prayer and room for silence. It has challenged us
to rediscover the central experience of Christianity.

There is a growing search for spirituality in the

Church today, a search which goes beyond programs and movements. It is a flowering of the
personal and communal concern to live the gospel
more deeply. The renewed liturgy, the revised
sacramental rites, the reemphasis on scripture,
are providing the context within which personal
faith and prayer can flourish. More and more
Christians are taking seriously the challenge to
clarify their values and to develop their sensitivity
to God's presence in their lives. They recognize
the need to balance science with faith, technology
with contemplation. They choose to explore the
world of inner space with the same intensity and
conviction that led others to leave the earth in
search of the stars.

But it is not just any spiritual vision that is
stirring in the Church today. It is a spirituality that
does not separate the sacred from the profane, the
body from the spirit, or the call to holiness from
the call to wholeness. It is a spirituality that
celebrates the mystery and sacredness of life in all
its dimensions. It is a spirituality that sees God in
snow patterns and in rush hour traffic. It is a
spirituality that enters the human in search of the
divine. It is, in a word, a spirituality which arises
from the paschal mystery as the central experience of the Christian gospel.

Dancing and Weeping: Accepting
the Human Paradox

Christian spirituality is a call to live in the real
world of human paradox. It is a choice to dance

and to weep as we journey toward God. Jesus did not come to solve the human dilemma; he came to *redeem* it and to make it life-giving. He did not save us *from* the human condition; he saved us *in* and *through* the human condition. There are more stables in Christianity than castles. There is more straw than satin. The treasure of the gospel is found in a field. It grows in the hearts of carpenters and fishermen. Jesus calls it forth in the lives of the blind and the lame, the tax collectors and the prostitutes. Today he calls *it* forth in the lives of the oppressed and the poor, the junkies and the inmates, the children who are abandoned and the widows who are lonely. The gospel celebrates the world of human beings who struggle and fail, who sin and repent, who are vulnerable to life and who smile through their tears.

Jesus redeemed human life by living it. He carried its contradictions to the cross. He raised up its promises in resurrection. In one journey through death to new life he transformed the meaning of human existence. His life spoke a simple message of trust in the Father and loving service toward his brothers and sisters.

In its simplicity, the gospel makes radical demands on our lives. Most of us are uneasy with the human condition. We are not comfortable with the paradoxical quality of our search. We attempt to solve the tension of the human dilemma instead of sharing the journey that redeems it. Our solution is to demand that life be either dancing or weeping, but not both. This is not really a solution.

When we divide them, our weeping becomes despair and our dancing becomes a selfish pursuit of happiness.

There are some who see life as pain-ridden and therefore futile. They try to cope with the darkness that surrounds them by withdrawing into themselves or by escaping into other-worldly experiences. They remain on the periphery of life, too bitter to see hope, too frightened to risk involvement.

There are others who attempt to solve the human paradox by pretending that suffering can be denied, or at least ignored. They believe that happiness is a commodity which can be purchased. They measure the "good life" in economic terms. This attitude is characteristic of a large part of our society today. It is supported and maintained by the world of advertising, which creates an ideal of affluence as the normal road to personal fulfillment. The media present us with images of attractive, healthy people who enjoy luxury in a setting of leisure. It is a world of consumer goods and conveniences. It is a world of deodorants and pain relievers, where medicine removes suffering and insurance buys security. It is a culture which creates expectations of success and good health, scholarships and promotions, fringe benefits and higher salaries. It is the good life for consumers, a retail version of salvation. But it is a world designed only for dancing. There is no room in it for tears, no script for failure, no place for suffering.

The Christian gospel cannot find a home in this version of the good life. Christianity is good news, but it is not easy news or comfortable news. The paschal mystery calls us to move beyond the wonderland of consumer goods and leisure time, to make a journey through the real world of broken promises and healed relationships. Christian life is a passage through the world of Monday mornings and lonely holidays, through the world of weddings and funerals, of honeymoons and nursing homes. It celebrates the miracle of birth, the struggle of growth and the fear of dying.

Christianity confronts us with the realization that we cannot create our own happiness nor can we purchase fulfillment with a credit card. We can only receive life as a gift from God. "We are God's work of art," writes St. Paul, "created in Christ Jesus to live *the good life* as from the beginning he had meant us to live it" (Ep. 2:10).

Christians who commit themselves to this gospel way of life experience their lives as signs of contradiction. Their way of life is an indictment of the superficial views that surround them. The Christian journey does not ignore the experience of suffering. It does not deny the reality of death. It walks through the darkness and is vulnerable to pain and failure. It celebrates the weeping as much as it does the dancing. It begins with the assumption that tension and uncertainty are as important to life as relaxation and security.

One of the most important roles for Christian spirituality today is the task of healing and integrating our vision of the human. The gospel challenges us to accept the paradoxical quality of human life, which so much of the rest of the world attempts to deny. To dance, to weep, to journey toward God. This is the Christian version of the good life.

Citizens and Exiles: Living with Ambiguity

The paradox of the gospel goes beyond the mystery of our personal journey. As Christians, we also approach the world around us in a spirit of creative tension. We are both patriots and rebels. We are both citizens of the earth and exiles of the kingdom. Christian life is a journey through the hills and valleys of creation. The journey is incarnational, but it does not permit us to settle down. The journey is transcendent, but it does not allow us to abandon the earth.

The Christian lives in the tension of accepting the world, and, at the same time, striving to transform it. Aware of this tension, St. Peter exhorts his fellow Christians: "I urge you, my dear people, while you are visitors and pilgrims, to keep yourselves free from the selfish passions that attack the soul" (I P 2:11). The Christian, as Chesterton once pointed out, is someone who hates the world enough to change it, and who loves the world enough to think that it is worth changing.

What is the reason for this ambiguous relationship with the world? The answer is deceptively simple. The basis for the ambiguity is related to

the struggle between God's redeeming love and
the brokenness of human life.

"And God saw that it was good." This is the
joyful refrain which echoes at the end of each day
of creation. Genesis pictures Yahweh creating the
world with loving care. Scripture celebrates creation as the overflow of God's beauty and goodness.

Evil enters the world only through human sinful-
ness. Adam and Eve refuse to accept the mystery
of the human condition. They refuse to live as
pilgrims who are dependent on a loving Father.
They turn from God, and the world becomes an
arena of evil and violence. Adam and Eve are
simply names for Everyman and Everywoman.
When human beings grasp at divinity instead of
accepting their dependence on God and on one
another, the world mirrors their rebellion. "Ac-
cursed be the soil because of you. With suffering
shall you get your food from it every day of your
life. It shall yield brambles and thistles, and you
shall eat wild plants. With sweat on your brow
shall you eat your bread until you return to the
soil, as you were taken from it. For dust you are
and to dust you shall return" (Gn 3:18-19). The
environmental crisis is not an exclusively modern
problem. It is the manifestation of the broken
relationship between human beings and their lack
of harmony with God and with the earth.

When Jesus begins his public ministry, the
world is dominated by darkness. Jesus comes out
of the desert and enters a world which is occupied
by the forces of evil. He confronts the blindness

and pride, the bitterness and violence of the
human heart. "Alas for the world because of such
obstacles," he cries out (Mt 18:7). Jesus declares
that the world which is created by human violence
and hypocrisy is evil. It is a world that rejects his
word and turns from his desire to heal it. The
presence of Christ is a judgment on this sin-
dominated world. "On these grounds is sentence
pronounced: that though the light has come into
the world men have shown they prefer darkness to
the light because their deeds were evil" (Jn 3:19).
Jesus tells his followers that they cannot depend
on the empty promises or the deceptive ways of
this world of darkness.

The New Testament writers echo this judgment
of Jesus. In sweeping terms, Paul describes the
ambiguity of being a Christian pilgrim in a passing
world: "Brothers, this is what I mean: our time is
growing short. Those who have wives should live
as though they had none, and those who mourn
should live as though they had nothing to mourn
for; those who are enjoying life should live as
though there were nothing to laugh about; those
whose life is buying things should live as though
they had nothing of their own; and those who have
to deal with the world should not become en-
grossed in it. I say this because the world as we
know it is passing away" (I Co 7:29-31).

The writings of John also reflect a suspicion of
the world and its powers of deception. "You must
not love this passing world or anything that is in
the world. The love of the Father cannot be in any

man who loves the world, because nothing the
world has to offer—the sensual body, the lustful
eye, pride in possessions—could ever come from
the Father but only from the world; and the world,
with all it craves for, is coming to an end; but
anyone who does the will of God remains forever"
(I Jn 2:15-17).

There are many Christians who misinterpret
and misuse these scriptural statements. They justify their desire to escape from the human condition and to avoid responsibility for history on the
grounds that scripture declares the world to be
evil. In doing so, they not only misinterpret the
Word of God, they also distort the significance of
the paschal journey of Christ. They deny the value
and meaning of the incarnation. They refuse to
share in the passover journey and to live with the
ambiguity of human experience.

The judgment of God stands against the world
which has been created by human violence and
oppression, but God's love for his creation is
irrevocable. "For the mountains may depart, the
hills be shaken, but my love for you will never
leave you and my covenant of peace with you will
never be shaken . . ." (Is 54:10).

At the moment we choose to condemn the world
as a place of evil, God chooses to love it and heal
it. When we seek to escape from the human
condition and from history, the Lord comes to take
its burden on his shoulders. When we seek for
ways to run from life, we encounter God coming to
embrace it. "Yes, God loved the world so much

that he gave his only Son, so that everyone who believes in him may not be lost but may have eternal life. For God sent his Son into the world not to condemn the world, but so that through him the world might be saved" (Jn 3:16-17).

God's last commentary on the world is one of love, not condemnation. The tragic character of human life arises from the ambiguous relationship which we have with the world. We are born into a world of illusion and prejudice, but it is a world which still struggles toward the truth. We grow up in a culture filled with deception and violence, but it is a culture which has been called to honesty and to peace. It is this world of brokenness and promise which God loves enough to redeem. It is the Lord himself who first walks the way of paradox. It is Jesus who redeems our ambiguities. It is the living God who loves us enough to forgive our contradictions and lead us to peace.

"And the Word became flesh and pitched his tent with us." For those who believe that the world is an illusion, this statement is an absurdity. For those who believe that the world is the final reality, this statement is irrelevant. But for those who believe that the Christian journey is the redemption of the world by love, it is the good news of salvation. It is the account of a God who is a pilgrim. It is the story of Jesus who is our Way. It is the story of those who follow the Way. It is our story. We are those who dance and weep. We are those who journey toward God.

NOTES

Chapter Two

[1] This story is based on similar illustrations collected by Martin Buber in his studies on the Hasidim. cf. *Tales of the Hasidim, The Early Masters,* Trans. by Olga Marx (New York: Schocken Books, 1947); and *The Legend of the Baal-Shem,* Trans. by Maurice S. Friedman (New York: Harper & Brothers, 1955).

[2] Saul D. Alinsky, *Reveille for Radicals* (New York: Vintage Books, 1969), p. 38.

[3] Theodore Roszak, *Where the Wasteland Ends* (Garden City, New York; Anchor Books, 1973), xvii.

Chapter Three

[1] Blaise Pascal, "The Memorial," as found in *The Essential Pascal,* edited by Robert W. Gleason, Trans. by G. F. Pullen (New York: New American Library, Mentor-Omega books, 1966) p. 205.

Chapter Four

[1] cf. Teilhard de Chardin, *The Future of Man,* Trans. by Norman Denny (New York & Evanston: Harper & Row, 1964), pp. 11-12.

Chapter Seven

[1] cf. Joseph Campbell, *Myths to Live By* (New York: Viking Press, 1972), pp. 202 ff. cf. also Campbell's other major works on myths, *The Masks of God,* and, *The Hero With a Thousand Faces.*

I am indebted to Gerald Vann, O.B., for many of the insights in this section. He develops the theme of Christ as hero in his book, *The Paradise Tree* (New York: Sheed and Ward, 1959).

Chapter Nine

[1] Nikos Kazantzakis, *Saint Francis,* Trans. by P. A. Bien (New York: Simon & Schuster, Touchstone Books, 1962) p. 187.